Informational Texts for
Striving Readers

High-Interest Nonfiction Passages
With Comprehension Questions

MICHAEL PRIESTLEY

■SCHOLASTIC
Teacher
RESOURCES

ACKNOWLEDGMENTS

For their assistance in the development of this book,
the author would like to acknowledge contributions
from Sheri Gushta, Claire Daniel, Cheryl Gracey,
and Lisa Moore.

Photos ©: Cover: Orion: NASA; Simone Biles: Tom Weller/Getty Images; 19: Jim McMahon/Mapman ®; 21: Mark Brake/Getty Images; 31: Amy Sanderson/ZUMA Wire/Alamy; 39: Historic Collection/Alamy; 42: Pictorial Press Ltd/Alamy; 50 (center): Warships/Alamy; (center right): David Wa/Alamy; (bottom): Jim McMahon/Mapman ®; 60: Tibrina Hobson/Getty Images; 75: NASA; 77: NASA; 79: Historic Collection/Alamy. All other photos Shutterstock.com.

Editor: Maria L. Chang
Cover design: Tannaz Fassihi
Interior design: Maria Lilja

ISBN: 978-1-338-71465-4
Scholastic Inc., 557 Broadway, New York, NY 10012
Copyright © 2021 by Michael Priestley
Published by Scholastic Inc. All rights reserved.
Printed in the U.S.A.
First printing, January 2021.
1 2 3 4 5 6 7 8 9 10   40   30 29 28 27 26 25 24 23 22 21

CONTENTS

Interpreting Information

Reasons and Evidence

Integrating Information

Social Studies and Science Texts

Practice Test

A NOTE TO TEACHERS

Welcome to *Informational Texts for Striving Readers: Grade 4*. Inside this book you'll find 30 reading passages designed to engage students and help increase their comprehension skills. The high-interest texts include a variety of informational articles and some literary nonfiction (see sidebar). All the passages feature grade-appropriate content written at relatively low readability levels, ranging from Grades 3.0 to 4.5 (between 500L and 750L, based on the Lexile measures). Generally, passages at the beginning are the easiest, with the difficulty level gradually increasing as you progress through the book.

The passages are organized in ten chapters that focus on core reading standards and comprehension skills. Each passage comes with comprehension questions in a variety of formats, including multiple choice, multiple response, short answer, two-part evidence-based, text highlighting (sometimes called "hotspot"), and matching/comparison tables. These questions help students think about what they have read and make sure they understand it. They also give students practice in answering various types of test questions. Even more important, they can give you assessment data to help you determine how well your students are reading or what kinds of instructional support they might need.

Quick Assessment

For additional assessment, a practice test follows the ten chapters. You'll find the answer key to both the comprehension questions and practice test at the back of the book. Item rationales, which explain why answer choices are correct or incorrect, are part of the answer key.

To score the questions, award each correct response with one point. A multiple-choice question is worth one point; a multiple-response item with two correct answers is worth two points. For two-part items, students must answer Part A correctly before they can earn credit for the correct response(s) in Part B. Matching and comparison tables are worth one point each if all answers within the item are correct. For short-answer questions, accept responses that vary from the exact wording in the answer key.

Taking It Further

You can also use some of the passages to have students go beyond answering the questions provided. For example, you might choose to have students write a summary of the text or compose an essay based on one or more passages. For the more challenging texts, students may benefit from discussing them first and then writing about them in a variety of ways.

> ### Informational Text and Literary Nonfiction
>
> **According to the Common Core State Standards, informational text "includes biographies and autobiographies; books about history, social studies, science, and the arts; technical texts, including directions, forms, and information displayed in graphs, charts, or maps; and digital sources on a range of topics" (ELA Standard 10: Range of Text Types for K–5). This broad definition also includes all literary nonfiction, such as personal essays, speeches, opinion pieces, and memoirs.**

Name: _____ Date: _____

What's a Pangolin?

1 Have you ever seen such a strange-looking animal? The pangolin is a mammal about the size of a dog. It has a long tail and sharp claws. It has a long tongue but no teeth. And unlike most mammals, the pangolin's body is covered with scales. They help protect this animal.

A pangolin is sometimes called a "scaly anteater."

2 Some pangolins live mostly in trees. Others live on the ground in burrows. All pangolins sleep during the day. They look for food at night. They eat mostly termites and ants. Pangolins use their claws to rip open nests. Then they slurp up the bugs with their tongues. Yum!

3 In the Malay language, *pangolin* means "roll over." When in danger, this animal rolls into a ball. And, like a skunk, it releases a strong smell to drive enemies away.

4 Sadly, these defenses do not protect pangolins from people. Hunters catch these animals and sell them for meat. They also sell the scales, which people in some countries use for medicine. Selling pangolins is against the law. That's because pangolins may be the most endangered animals on the planet. The United Nations and other groups are working to save the pangolins.

---

1. A pangolin is most like what other animal?

   (A) dog   (C) termite

   (B) skunk   (D) anteater

2. When in danger, what does a pangolin do to protect itself? Choose two answers.

   (A) It runs away.   (D) It goes underground.

   (B) It rolls into a ball.   (E) It lets out a strong smell.

   (C) It climbs up a tree.

3. In some countries, what do people use pangolin scales for?

_____

Name: _____ Date: _____

Hello, Robot!

1   Ms. Dali is a teacher in Alabama. She is getting ready for a new school year. She sits at her computer to shop for school supplies. She chooses pencils, chalk, glue, and notebooks. Then she clicks on a button that says, "Place this order." This sets robots into action!

2   Ms. Dali's order goes to a warehouse in Utah. That is hundreds of miles away. There, a "picker" robot zooms along steel tracks. It stops above a large crate. Then it reaches down with a metal arm. It picks up a package of pencils. It puts the pencils in a cart for Ms. Dali. The robot finds her items one by one. Each item goes into the cart.

A robot arm picks packages from shelves in a warehouse.

3   Before long, Ms. Dali's order is filled. Next, the cart goes to a "packer" robot. This robot finds a box that is just the right size. It puts the items into the box. A third robot tapes the box shut. Then it adds a shipping label and pushes the box onto a belt.

4   The box goes to the shipping area. There, it goes onto a truck. The truck takes the box to a plane, and the plane flies it to Alabama. Then the box goes into a van. A person drives the van to Ms. Dali's school. The package arrives—in one day!

Hello, Robot!

1. **Where does Ms. Dali live?**

    _____

2. **What does Ms. Dali buy from her computer?**

    (A) food items   (C) books

    (B) new clothes   (D) things for school

3. **What makes the "picker" robot start working?**

    (A) Ms. Dali places an order.

    (B) A metal arm reaches down.

    (C) Ms. Dali gets ready for school.

    (D) The box goes onto a big truck.

4. **Underline two sentences from paragraph 3 that tell what the "packer" robot does.**

        Before long, Ms. Dali's order is filled. Next, the cart goes to a "packer" robot. This robot finds a box that is just the right size. It puts the items into the box. A third robot tapes the box shut. Then it adds a shipping label and pushes the box onto a belt.

5. **How does the box go from Utah to Alabama?**

    (A) by van   (C) by truck

    (B) by cart   (D) by plane

Name: _____ Date: _____

What Makes a Champion?

Informational Texts for Striving Readers: Grade 4 © 2021 by Michael Priestley, Scholastic Inc. • page 9

1   Do you know what you want to be when you grow up? Cori Gauff has known since she was 8 years old. She wanted to be the best tennis player in the world.

2   Cori, who goes by "Coco," was born in Florida in 2004. By age 7, she was playing tennis all the time. She worked hard. Soon, she started winning. At 13, she became the youngest girl ever to play in top tournaments. One was the U.S. Open. It is one of the biggest. It is held every year in New York. The next year, she won the junior girls' title in the French Open.

Coco started playing tennis when she was 6 years old.

3   As she won more matches, her parents began to worry. She could soon be famous. Would she be able to handle life in the spotlight? Her father, Corey, was her coach. He helped her learn how to handle the attention.

4   Her mother, Candi, helped, too. Before games, Coco's mom would tell her, "Don't make things bigger than they are. Pretend you're at home playing with a friend."

5   In 2019, Coco played in the world tennis championship at Wimbledon. That is in England. It is one of the top contests in the world. She was just 15. Huge crowds were watching. But she stayed calm. She just told herself that the tennis court was the same size as the ones back home.

6   Nobody expected Coco to do very well at Wimbledon. But she surprised them all. Coco beat some well-known players. She even beat one of her heroes, Venus Williams. Venus had won the event five times! Coco said that her goal was just to play her best. And she did.

7   Months later, Coco beat Venus again. Tennis fans cheered for her. Coco Gauff became the player everyone wanted to watch.

What Makes a Champion?

1. **Where was Coco born?**

   (A) New York   (C) England

   (B) Florida   (D) France

2. **At age 8, what did Coco want to be?**

   _____

3. **Who is Coco's coach?**

   (A) her father   (C) her brother

   (B) her mother   (D) Venus Williams

4. **What did Coco's parents worry about when she started winning? Underline the sentence that tells what they worried about.**

   As she won more matches, her parents began to worry. She could soon be famous. Would she be able to handle life in the spotlight? Her father, Corey, was her coach. He helped her learn how to handle the attention.

5. **What was Coco's goal at her first Wimbledon?**

   (A) to win every game   (C) to beat Venus Williams

   (B) to play her best   (D) to meet well-known players

Name: _____   Date: _____

What Do Presidents Eat?

1   If you were dining with the president of the United States, what would you expect to eat? How about some squirrel stew? That was a favorite of James A. Garfield, our 20th president. James Madison was president in the 1800s. He liked to serve oyster ice cream.

2   Most of the time, White House chefs cook the president's meals. Presidents often have important guests come to dinner. They plan fancy meals to show off the best American foods.

3   But some presidents went to the kitchen themselves. Dwight Eisenhower was one. He loved to cook. He sometimes made up his own recipes. He once made his own version of green turtle soup. He served it to the leaders of Canada and Mexico. (There's no record of whether they liked it.)

Cottage cheese with ketchup was a favorite snack of two U.S. presidents.

4   Presidents' private meals are different from what they eat in public. The chefs serve whatever they want. If the president wants peanut butter and jelly, a chef will make it. Presidents often ask for plain foods or things they ate when growing up. For example, Richard Nixon liked cottage cheese with ketchup. So did Gerald Ford. Jimmy Carter often enjoyed a bowl of grits. That was a favorite food back in his home state. Ronald Reagan was known for snacking on jellybeans. He kept a bowl of them on his desk.

5   Abe Lincoln didn't care much about food. He often forgot to eat. When he did eat, though, he enjoyed plain cornbread with honey. Perhaps it reminded him of his home back in Illinois.

What Do Presidents Eat?

1. **What is the main idea of this passage?**

   (A) Presidents have important guests.

   (B) Foods have changed since the 1800s.

   (C) Most presidents like to eat fancy foods.

   (D) Some presidents choose surprising foods.

2. **Name two examples of foods that U.S. presidents have served to their guests.**

   _____

3. **Put an X in the correct box beside each president to show what food he liked.**

President	cottage cheese	grits	jellybeans	squirrel stew
Jimmy Carter				
Gerald Ford				
James A. Garfield				
Richard Nixon				
Ronald Reagan				

4. **How was Lincoln different from most other presidents?**

   (A) He liked to cook.

   (B) He did not eat soup.

   (C) He often forgot to eat.

   (D) He ate meals in the kitchen.

5. **Which sentence in paragraph 2 tells why presidents choose certain foods for their guests? Underline the sentence.**

   Most of the time, White House chefs cook the president's meals. Presidents often have important guests come to dinner. They plan fancy meals to show off the best American foods.

Name: _____ Date: _____

The Changing Coast Guard

1 Who catches smugglers, rescues ships in trouble, tracks icebergs, and protects the ocean? If you said the U.S. Coast Guard (USCG), you're right!

2 The U.S. Coast Guard wasn't always called the "Coast Guard." It has had other names. But its jobs keep changing. And the name has changed to fit the jobs.

3 The USCG started in 1790. At first, it was called the Revenue Cutter Service. *Revenue* means "money." Cutters were small, fast ships. Back then, smugglers used boats to sneak goods into the country. They did not want to pay taxes. But our nation needed money from those taxes. The cutters' job was to catch the smugglers. This is still a major job for the Coast Guard. And some of their ships are still called cutters.

The U.S. Coast Guard uses helicopters and ships to help people in danger.

4 Sometimes ships at sea get in trouble. In the early 1800s, lifeboat stations were built along the shore to help them. The stations had boats, ropes, and other rescue tools. In 1878, many rescue groups joined to become one agency. It was called the Life-Saving Service. Then, in 1915, it joined with the Revenue Cutter Service. Together, they became the Coast Guard. They rescued people and ships from danger.

5 Lighthouses also help keep ships safe. They are built along the coasts. They warn sailors to stay away from dangers, such as rocks. In this way, they help prevent shipwrecks. America has had lighthouses since 1716. In 1789, the first U.S. Congress set up the Lighthouse Service. That group became part of the USCG in 1939. Today's Coast Guard also helps protect ships. It provides things like buoys, maps, and weather warnings.

6 In time of war, the USCG acts as part of the Navy. At all other times, it works by itself.

(continued)

7   Members of the modern Coast Guard have many other jobs. They track icebergs. They help protect the ocean. They teach people about safe boating. They now use planes and helicopters as well as ships. They work on lakes and rivers, too, not just on the sea. Their name has not changed for a while, though. The Coast Guard is still the Coast Guard.

1.   **What is the main idea of this passage?**

  (A) The USCG started out as the Revenue Cutter Service.

  (B) Today's Coast Guard does more than just guard coasts.

  (C) As the Coast Guard's jobs have changed, so has its name.

  (D) Protecting ships from danger is a job for the Coast Guard.

2.   **What was the main job of the Revenue Cutter Service?**

  _____

3.   **What is the main topic of paragraph 4?**

  (A) life-saving groups   (C) tools used for rescues

  (B) ships at sea   (D) Coast Guard cutters

4.   **What tools does the modern Coast Guard have that the earlier services did not? Choose <u>two</u> answers.**

  (A) maps   (D) helicopters

  (B) cutters   (E) lighthouses

  (C) planes

5.   **Which sentence in the last paragraph best supports the idea that the Coast Guard does not just work in the oceans?**

  _____

  _____

Name: _____   Date: _____

Wild Ponies of Chincoteague

1   For hundreds of years, wild ponies have lived on Assateague Island in Virginia. No one knows for sure how they got there. Some people think the first ponies came from a Spanish ship that wrecked in the 1500s. Others say that in the 1700s farmers took some ponies to the island to graze. Either way, the horses made the island their home. But no people live there.

Every summer, ponies swim from Assateague Island to nearby Chincoteague Island.

2   Over time, the herd size grew. Ponies sometimes swam across to Chincoteague, a nearby island. People who lived on the island kept some of the horses and put them in pens. They returned the rest to Assateague. Penning some of the horses kept the herd from getting too big for the island. Too many horses on the island would mean not enough grass to eat.

Pony Penning

3   Putting the ponies into pens became a yearly event. People from all over the country would come and enjoy a day of fun. Then, in 1924, the Chincoteague firefighters got an idea. They needed to raise money for a new fire engine. They decided to sell some ponies from the herd. They put together a carnival to draw more people. The festival was so successful that the firefighters decided to do it again every year.

(continued)

Visitor Information

Parking is scarce. Visitors may take a bus to Pony Swim Lane.

Wear old clothes and shoes. The viewing area is very muddy.

Several companies offer boat rides out to watch the ponies.

No pets are allowed.

The Pony Festival

4   The festival starts just before the Fourth of July. On weekends, people can enjoy rides, games, and food. Fireworks on the Fourth are part of the fun.

5   Toward the end of July, the "Saltwater Cowboys" go to work. They sail over to Assateague Island and round up adult ponies and young ones born in the spring. The cowboys move them into a corral. Then a vet checks all the ponies.

6   Near the end of the month, the big day arrives. The cowboys check the weather and the currents. Then they release the ponies. They let the ponies swim across to Chincoteague. There, the cowboys hold an auction. They sell as many of the ponies as they can. Any ponies left after the auction swim back to their home. There's always next year!

1. **What is the main idea of this passage?**

   (A) Pony-penning events last for a whole month.

   (B) Assateague ponies are well suited to the island.

   (C) People on Chincoteague Island have a pony festival every year.

   (D) Ponies have lived on Assateague Island for a long time without people.

2. **According to the passage, how did the first ponies get to Assateague Island? Give _two_ answers.**

   _____

   _____

3. **Which sentence from paragraph 3 tells how the pony auction got started?**

   _____

   _____

4. **What is the main topic of the sidebar, "Visitor Information"?**

   (A) where to park for the festival   (C) what to wear to the festival

   (B) what people coming for   (D) where to buy a wild pony
        the festival should know

Name: _____ Date: _____

Frankenstorm!

1 Just before Halloween in 2012, a giant storm crept up the East Coast of the United States. Because of the date, people called it "Frankenstorm." Its official name was Hurricane Sandy. It was supposed to move safely out to the Atlantic Ocean. But it didn't.

2 Scientists are usually good at predicting hurricanes. They use computers to figure out where storms will go. They look at water temperatures and wind speeds. They look at air pressure and moisture levels. They even consider the phases of the moon. They use all this information from past storms to develop models. These models help predict what will happen.

Hurricane Sandy was the most destructive storm of 2012.

3 But sometimes models can be wrong. This was the case with Sandy. U.S. computer models said that the storm would head out to sea. It would fade away. But European models predicted that Sandy would take a left turn and hit land. They were right. On October 29, Sandy struck New York City and New Jersey, and it struck hard.

4 Hurricane Sandy was more than 900 miles across. The moon was full, so ocean tides were high. These factors made Sandy very powerful. People were not prepared. They believed the U.S. models. Sandy caused more than $70 billion in damages and claimed many lives.

5 Some people blamed the scientists. They used old computers and did not have the best software. A year later, weather centers had new computers and new software. Now they can predict the path of major storms better than ever.

Frankenstorm!

1. **Why was Hurricane Sandy so powerful?**

    (A) Computers used information from past storms.

    (B) It was called "Frankenstorm."

    (C) The storm was huge, and the tide was high.

    (D) It struck just before Halloween.

2. **Where did U.S. computer models predict Sandy would go?**

    _____

3. **Which sentence from paragraph 4 describes the effects of Hurricane Sandy? Underline the sentence.**

    Hurricane Sandy was more than 900 miles across. The moon was full, so ocean tides were high. These factors made Sandy very powerful. People were not prepared. They believed the U.S. models. Sandy caused more than $70 billion in damages and claimed many lives.

4. **Why weren't people prepared when Hurricane Sandy struck the U.S.?**

    (A) The full moon caused the tides to rise.

    (B) Scientists made the wrong predictions.

    (C) The storm was more than 900 miles wide.

    (D) New computers did not work as well as the old ones.

Name: _____ Date: _____

Taming a River

1   The mighty Colorado River starts up in the Rocky Mountains. For ages, the river flooded in the spring when winter snow melted. It dried up in the summer when there was no rain. In 1905, the river overflowed. It flooded the valleys in Southern California. A wall of water washed away farms. It knocked down homes and ruined cities. Something had to be done.

The Colorado River flows through five U.S. states and into Mexico.

2   Engineers suggested building dams along the river. Dams would form lakes to store water in the spring. Then the water could be released slowly in the summer. That would help farmers. Controlling the river would stop the floods. It would also make electric power for homes and factories.

3   In 1931, the U.S. government decided to build a dam in Boulder Canyon. It would block the river where it flowed through Arizona into Nevada.

4   Building the dam would be dangerous work. But people needed jobs. Workers came from around the country. They needed a place to live, so they built Boulder City nearby. They put in a road from the city to the river. They built railroad lines to carry supplies.

5   To build the dam, workers had to move the Colorado River out of the way. They blasted tunnels through rock walls. As the tunnels opened, the river flowed in new directions. The old riverbed dried up. They could start building the dam.

6   Workers stacked 215 huge concrete blocks in columns. The concrete used in the dam was enough to build a sidewalk around the earth! That much concrete normally would take 100 years to cool. But workers built one-inch pipes into the blocks. Then they ran ice water through the pipes. This cooled the concrete blocks in less than two months. Then workers used grout to seal the spaces between the blocks. The dam became a solid, one-piece wall.

(continued)

7   When the dam was ready, water from the river was sent back toward the dam. This formed Lake Mead behind the wall. In June 1935, a great flood raced down the river and roared through the canyons. The dam held back the water. The project was a success! Today, the dam is known as Hoover Dam.

1. **Why did the government decide to build a dam on the Colorado River?**

   (A) Some states wanted to have more electricity.

   (B) The river often flooded in spring and then dried up.

   (C) Many people needed jobs.

   (D) The river flowed from snow in the Rocky Mountains.

2. **What step did workers take <u>before</u> the building of the dam began?**

   (A) They built a city for workers.

   (B) They cooled the concrete.

   (C) They made stacks of huge blocks.

   (D) They built pipes into the blocks.

3. **How did workers move the Colorado River so they could build Hoover Dam?**

   _____

   _____

4. **While building the dam, workers ran ice water through pipes to —**

   (A) create a lake   (C) slow down the river

   (B) cool the concrete   (D) seal spaces between the blocks

5. **How did Hoover Dam fix the problems the river was causing?**

   (A) It stopped snow from melting into the river.

   (B) It kept parts of the Colorado River dry.

   (C) It created a lake to control water flow.

   (D) It gave jobs to people who needed work.

Name: _____ Date: _____

"Koala! Find!"

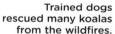

1   Taylor is a young English springer spaniel. This 4-year-old dog is a hero. She helped save several koalas from wildfires in Australia.

2   In Australia, summer starts in December. By then, the hot, dry season is already underway. In 2019, temperatures in parts of Australia were the hottest ever. The land was very dry. Fires broke out all over the state of New South Wales.

3   With strong winds to spread them, the fires burned for nearly four months. They were the worst wildfires in Australia's history. Millions of acres burned. People had to leave their homes for the safety of beaches. There was nothing on the sand that would burn.

Trained dogs rescued many koalas from the wildfires.

4   Thousands of animals also tried to escape the fires. People found injured kangaroos and koalas along the roads. They wrapped the animals in blankets and took them to animal hospitals.

5   But many other animals stayed in the bushlands, where the fires had been. Frightened koalas searched for food there. Koalas eat only the leaves of eucalyptus trees. But the fires had burned all the trees. Thanks to Taylor and other very special dogs, many of the koalas were found and saved.

6   Rescuers trained Taylor to find kangaroos, koalas, foxes, and other animals. When she went to work, the team of people she worked with told her what to look for.

7   At the command "Koala! Find!" Taylor raced off into the burned bushland. She sniffed for the scent of koalas. The frightened animals were often clinging to tree branches. When she smelled a koala, she sat or lay down. This alerted her handlers. They knew a koala was nearby. They passed the word to expert koala spotters. Then the spotters rescued the hungry animals. For her work, Taylor got a reward, like a treat or a ball.

8   In February 2020, heavy rains finally ended the spread of fires in New South Wales. Rescue animals like Taylor got some rest. But their jobs weren't done. Taylor and other special animals like her will always have important work to do.

"Koala! Find!"

1. **What caused the fires in Australia to get so big?**

   (A) The weather was hot and windy.

   (B) The fires started in November.

   (C) People had to leave their homes.

   (D) Animals could not find food.

2. **Which sentence from paragraph 3 tells why people went to beaches to escape the fires? Write the sentence.**

   _____

   _____

3. **Why did people take dogs to the bushland to find koalas?**

   (A) People wanted to move the koalas to beaches.

   (B) Dogs needed practice finding injured animals.

   (C) Koalas were in danger and needed help.

   (D) There were no more injured animals on the roads.

4. **This question has two parts. Answer Part A. Then answer Part B.**

   PART A **How did workers find koalas in the bushland?**

   (A) They used cameras to see the koalas.

   (B) Dogs located the koalas by smell.

   (C) They climbed trees to look for koalas.

   (D) Dogs drove the koalas out of the trees.

   PART B **Which sentence best supports the answer to Part A?**

   (A) "Rescuers trained Taylor to find kangaroos, koalas, foxes, and other animals."

   (B) "They passed the word to expert koala spotters."

   (C) "She sniffed for the scent of koalas."

   (D) "The frightened animals were often clinging to tree branches."

Name: _____ Date: _____

Visiting Mars

1   On some nights, you can look up at the sky and see Mars. It is a reddish planet. It is very cold and covered with dust and dirt. Like Earth, it has flat plains and tall mountains. It also has places that look like they were carved by rivers or streams. Could there have been water on Mars?

2   Since 1997, NASA has sent five "rovers" to Mars to study the planet. A *rover* is a robot vehicle. Scientists at NASA use computers to **control** these rovers from Earth. The first was called *Sojourner*. It weighed 23 pounds. It had six wheels so it could move around.

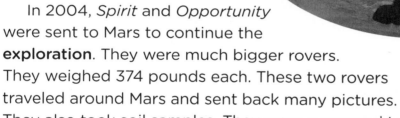

3   In 2004, *Spirit* and *Opportunity* were sent to Mars to continue the **exploration**. They were much bigger rovers. They weighed 374 pounds each. These two rovers traveled around Mars and sent back many pictures.

A rover allows scientists to explore a planet without having to send humans.

They also took soil samples. They were supposed to work for about 90 days, but they lasted much longer. *Spirit* **operated** for six years. *Opportunity* set a record by working for 15 years. Its time ended in 2019.

4   Both of these rovers found evidence that Mars once had water on it. That means there may have been some form of life on the planet. They also found old volcanoes.

5   In 2012, the fourth rover landed on Mars. It is called *Curiosity*. It weighs almost 2,000 pounds. Its **mission** is to find out if Mars once had life.

6   The fifth and largest rover was **launched** in 2020 for a landing in 2021. Its name is *Perseverance*. Its job is to see if the planet can support human life. If so, then humans might one day go to Mars.

Visiting Mars

1. **Which phrase gives a clue to the meaning of *control* as it is used in paragraph 2?**

   (A) "to study"   (C) "from Earth"

   (B) "use computers"   (D) "move around"

2. **Write a phrase from paragraph 3 that gives a clue to the meaning of *exploration*.**

   _____

   _____

3. **What does the word *operated* mean in paragraph 3?**

   (A) sent   (C) ended

   (B) took   (D) worked

4. **Which word means about the same as *mission* as it is used in paragraph 5?**

   (A) job   (C) sample

   (B) rover   (D) vehicle

5. **What is the meaning of the word *launched* in the last paragraph?**

   (A) turned on   (C) sent into space

   (B) planned for   (D) built for a purpose

Name: _____ Date: _____

The Great Sphinx

1   Near the city of Giza in Egypt sits a huge statue. It has the body of a lion and the head of a man. It is called the Great Sphinx. It is 240 feet long and 66 feet high. Workers carved the whole thing from one mound of stone. It is one of the world's largest stone sculptures.

2   Many **archaeologists** have studied the Great Sphinx. They believe it was made around 2500 BCE. It is a great example of art from the Egyptian **civilization**. Most experts agree that the statue has the face of King Khafre. He was the ruler of Egypt at that time. The statue has a royal headdress that only a **noble** person would wear.

Until the early 1800s, the Great Sphinx was buried up to its shoulders in sand.

3   The Sphinx sits near a number of stone pyramids. Some of the pyramids were built as tombs, or graves. The bodies of great kings were placed in them when they died. But no one is sure about the purpose of the Great Sphinx. It was probably built as a **tribute** to King Khafre to honor his greatness.

4   According to one **prophecy**, the Sphinx had a hidden room under it. In 1998, that room would open. It would hold a great secret about the world. But that prediction did not come true. The year 1998 came and went, but no room was found.

5   Over the years, the Sphinx has had a lot of damage. It was likely painted at one time. But only small traces of paint remain. The most obvious damage is the missing nose. It was knocked off or it fell off long ago. But the Great Sphinx is still one of the wonders of the world.

The Great Sphinx

1. **What is the meaning of the word *archaeologists* in paragraph 2?**

   (A) artists who carve stone   (C) people who study ancient ruins

   (B) workers who build things   (D) scientists who explore other countries

2. **What is the meaning of the word *civilization* in paragraph 2?**

   (A) a large city   (C) a form of government

   (B) advanced way of life   (D) land used for farming

3. **Which word in paragraph 2 means about the same as *noble*?**

   (A) "great"   (C) "statue"

   (B) "example"   (D) "royal"

4. **Write a phrase from paragraph 3 that gives a clue to the meaning of *tribute*.**

   _____

   _____

5. **Find a word in paragraph 4 that means about the same as *prophecy*. Underline the word.**

   According to one **prophecy**, the Sphinx had a hidden room under it. In 1998, that room would open. It would hold a great secret about the world. But that prediction did not come true. The year 1998 came and went, but no room was found.

Name: _____ Date: _____

The Greatest Outdoor Show on Earth

1   Welcome to the "Greatest Outdoor Show on Earth"! This fun-filled event happens every July in the city of Calgary in Alberta, Canada. It is called the Calgary Stampede.

2   The Stampede starts with a huge parade. Hundreds of horses and thousands of people march down the avenue. There are also dozens of floats and marching bands. Rodeo events begin on the second day. The midway opens up with games and rides. The barns fill with animals and farming **exhibits**. Country-music stars put on concerts.

A cowboy tries to stay on a wild horse.

3   Alberta, Canada, has many ranches and farms. A lot of cowboys and cowgirls live and work there. Every year, they go to the Stampede to compete for prizes in rodeo events. The total **value** of the prizes is more than two million dollars.

4   These **athletic** events take a lot of skill and strength. Some cowboys ride huge bulls or untamed horses called *broncos*. The winner is the rider who stays on the animal longest. Some cowboys have to catch a steer and **wrestle** it to the ground. Some men compete in calf roping. Women ride horses through a tough course in barrel racing. There is even a fun race for chuck wagons. In the old days, a cook drove the chuck wagon. This wagon was filled with food and pots and pans. It served as a kitchen for making meals for the cowboys.

5   Thousands of **tourists** come to see the sights and have fun. The Stampede lasts for ten days. It is the biggest event of the year in Calgary.

The Greatest Outdoor Show on Earth

1. **What is the meaning of the word *exhibits* in paragraph 2?**

    (A) tools

    (B) shows

    (C) classes

    (D) helpers

2. **Which phrase in paragraph 3 gives a clue to the meaning of *value*?**

    (A) "to compete"

    (B) "rodeo events"

    (C) "of the prizes"

    (D) "two million dollars"

3. **Write a phrase from paragraph 4 that gives a clue to the meaning of *athletic*.**

    _____

    _____

4. **What is the meaning of the word *wrestle* in paragraph 4?**

    (A) hold on

    (B) roll over

    (C) pull down

    (D) tie with rope

5. **Which phrase from the last paragraph gives a clue to the meaning of *tourists*?**

    (A) "lasts for ten days"

    (B) "to see the sights"

    (C) "have fun"

    (D) "biggest event of the year"

Name: _____ Date: _____

A Buried City

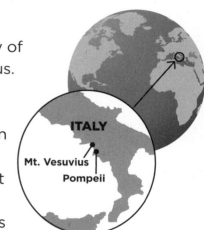

1   Almost 2,000 years ago, a huge explosion shook the city of Pompeii, Italy. It came from a volcano named Mt. Vesuvius.

2   When the volcano first erupted, it blew clouds of ash into the sky. The ash was so thick that it blocked the sunlight. Everything went dark. Then the ash rained down on the city. It buried everything, including people, shops, houses, and the baths. (Public baths were popular at that time.) Some people escaped, but most did not. Several feet of hot ash soon covered the entire city. Deadly gases from the volcano filled the air. The city was destroyed.

3   Some people returned to Pompeii soon after the eruption. But they could not dig through the huge piles of ash. So they left the city forever.

4   Over hundreds of years, people forgot about Pompeii. Life went on in nearby towns and cities. Then, in 1748, people started exploring the area. They uncovered items that had been hidden for centuries. As a result, they learned about the city and the people who had lived there.

Pompeii was about five miles from Mt. Vesuvius.

5   After the ash fell on the city, it hardened. Because the objects under the hard ash were protected from rain and sunlight, they stayed in excellent shape. Scientists uncovered a scene that was frozen in time. They found everyday items in the streets, such as pots and tools. Inside the houses were paintings in full color, pottery, jewelry, and coins. They even found loaves of bread in a bakery oven!

6   Based on what scientists found, Pompeii was clearly an active place. About 12,000 people lived in the city itself. Many of the people were rich. They lived in fancy homes. They owned beautiful art and gold jewelry. Pompeii had many shops, restaurants, and markets. The city even had an arena with almost 20,000 seats.

(continued)

7   Today, people can visit Pompeii to tour the ruins and see what life was like. About 2.5 million people visit every year. It has become a large museum. Historians have worked hard to keep the city of Pompeii safe from people and weather. Many items found in the city have been put in glass cases. Some have been covered in plaster to keep them safe. Special roofs have been built to keep rainwater away.

1. How does the author organize most of the information in this passage?

- **A** by explaining a problem and how it was solved
- **B** by describing an event and what happened as a result
- **C** by asking questions about an event and giving answers
- **D** by comparing life in the past to the life of today

2. What were <u>two</u> effects of the volcano erupting?

- **A** Ash darkened the sky.
- **B** People ran toward Pompeii.
- **C** Many people died in Pompeii.
- **D** A baker put loaves in the oven.
- **E** The government of Italy closed Pompeii.

3. Why did people stop living in Pompeii after the eruption?

- **A** They were scared of the volcano.
- **B** They had no money to return.
- **C** Their paintings were destroyed.
- **D** Thick layers of ash buried the city.

4. Which sentence in paragraph 5 tells why everyday items found in Pompeii were in such good condition? Write the sentence.

_____

_____

5. Today, thousands of people visit Pompeii to —

- **A** look for coins and jewelry
- **B** see how people lived long ago
- **C** watch the volcano explode again
- **D** enjoy the shops, restaurants, and markets

Informational Texts for Striving Readers: Grade 4 © 2021 by Michael Priestley, Scholastic Inc. • page 30

Name: _____ Date: _____

Flipping for Simone Biles

1   Simone Biles started by tumbling across the floor. Then she launched her body high into the air. She did a series of twists and flips in midair before landing back on her feet!

Simone Biles is the most decorated American gymnast.

2   Biles may be the world's greatest gymnast. She has won more medals than any other gymnast. As of 2020, Biles had taken home 30 medals. Nineteen of them were gold!

3   Simone was born in 1997. She grew up in Texas with her grandparents. When she was 6 years old, Simone went on a field trip to a gymnastics center. The coaches saw Simone copying the older kids. They urged Simone's family to let her take gymnastics lessons. It was clear she had natural talent.

4   Simone started lessons in 2003 at the same gym. She worked very hard. She wowed her coaches with her powerful twists and flips. Simone spent many full days at the gym to practice. She was schooled at home to allow time for training.

5   By 2011, Biles was one of the top gymnasts in the sport. In 2013, she competed in her first World Championship. She won first place all-around. This means she got the highest score in four different events. These included balance beam, uneven bars, floor exercise, and vault. She was the first African-American woman to win the all-around title.

5   At the 2016 Olympic Games, Biles won five medals. She was the first U.S. woman to win four gold medals. Then she was named Athlete of the Year. She was only 19 years old. And she's already looking forward to the next competition.

Flipping for Simone Biles

1. **How did Simone Biles first get interested in gymnastics?**

   Ⓐ She grew up in Texas.   Ⓒ She practiced at home.

   Ⓑ She went on a field trip.   Ⓓ She copied the older kids.

2. **This question has two parts. Answer Part A and then answer Part B.**

   PART A

   What structure does the author use to organize information in this passage?

   Ⓐ time order   Ⓒ problem and solution

   Ⓑ cause and effect   Ⓓ comparison and contrast

   PART B

   Which sentences from the passage support the answer to Part A? Choose <u>two</u> answers.

   Ⓐ "Biles may be the world's greatest gymnast."

   Ⓑ "The coaches saw Simone copying the older kids."

   Ⓒ "Simone started lessons in 2003 at the same gym."

   Ⓓ "By 2011, Biles was one of the top gymnasts in the sport."

   Ⓔ "She was the first U.S. woman to win four gold medals."

3. **What happened after Biles won her first World Championship?**

   Ⓐ She took first place in the all-around event.

   Ⓑ She was schooled at home by her parents.

   Ⓒ She took lessons at a gymnastic center.

   Ⓓ She won five medals at the Olympic Games.

Name: _____ Date: _____

Are We There Yet?

1   In many parts of the United States, a sure sign of fall is the honking sound
of Canada geese. As the weather gets colder, the geese fly south to warmer
places. In the spring, they fly north again.

2   Many kinds of animals migrate
every year. These include lots
of birds, fish, and even sea
turtles. But why do they travel
from one part of the world
to another? How do they
know the right way to go?
And which animals travel farthest?

Flying in V formation helps
geese save energy and keep
track of one another.

Why Animals Migrate

3   There are many reasons why animals migrate.
Most animals travel to find food or to give birth.
Many birds move each season to find the insects and other
foods they eat. For example, some birds eat caterpillars. They can
find caterpillars in northern places in the spring but not in winter,
so they fly south.

4   Both sea turtles and some fish, such as salmon, migrate to give birth.
They return to the same beach or stream where they were born. They lay
eggs in that same place, and then they leave.

How They Know the Way

5   Scientists are not completely sure how animals know which way to go
when they migrate. But they know that the earth has a strong magnetic
pull near each pole. Both birds and butterflies seem to use that magnetic
pull to find their direction.

6   Unlike birds, fish may use a sense of smell to find their way home. When
they are born, they learn what the water in that place smells like. When they
migrate later in life, they follow that smell.

(continued)

7   But many animals, such as loggerhead turtles, know their migration routes from birth. Every new generation of animals follows the same route by instinct. It is just something they are born with.

Animals That Travel Farthest

8   Scientists have studied many animals to see how far they travel. In Antarctica, penguins swim a few hundred miles to their breeding grounds. Canada geese fly several hundred miles every year. Flocks of monarch butterflies migrate from the Great Lakes to Mexico. They fly about 2,500 miles. Storks and swallows fly about 6,000 miles from northern Europe to southern Africa.

9   Certain sea creatures do some serious traveling. Some loggerhead turtles, for example, live near Japan. They swim 8,000 miles across the Pacific Ocean to lay eggs. Then they turn around and swim back. Leatherback sea turtles travel even farther. Most of them swim about 10,000 miles a year to find the jellyfish they like to eat. One turtle that scientists named Yoshi set a record by swimming 22,000 miles!

10   That is a remarkable distance. But it's not the farthest. The award for longest migration goes to the Arctic tern. This sea bird flies to the Arctic to lay eggs and then flies south to Antarctica. That trip can be as long as 51,000 miles—every year! That's a long way.

Are We There Yet?

1. **Why do most animals migrate? Give <u>two</u> reasons.**

   _____

   _____

2. **What text structure does the author use in the section titled "Why Animals Migrate"?**

   A time order   **C** problem and solution

   B cause and effect   **D** comparison and contrast

3. **This question has two parts. Answer Part A. Then answer Part B.**

   PART A

   What text structure does the author use in the section titled "Animals That Travel Farthest"?

   A time order   **C** problem and solution

   B cause and effect   **D** comparison and contrast

   PART B

   Which sentence from the passage supports the answer to Part A?

   A "Scientists have studied many animals to see how far they travel."

   B "Canada geese fly several hundred miles every year."

   C "Leatherback sea turtles travel even farther."

   D "That is a remarkable distance."

4. **In what way are birds and butterflies alike?**

   A They eat bugs and caterpillars.

   B They use a sense of smell to migrate.

   C They lay eggs in the place they were born.

   D They use Earth's magnetic pull to find their way.

5. **Which of these travels farthest every year?**

   A penguin   **C** Canada goose

   B Arctic tern   **D** loggerhead turtle

Name: _____ Date: _____

Read both texts about a special baseball game. Then answer the questions.

TEXT A
Civil War Baseball Game

1   **Baltimore, MD** — Baseball is catching on. Even as this war continues, our brave Union soldiers are spreading the sport wherever they go. The boys at Hilton Head, South Carolina, played a game on Christmas Day, 1862. Reports say that 40,000 people watched the contest. Our troops enjoyed a holiday from their duties. Families, local workers, and even prisoners went to watch.

2   Both teams were from New York regiments. One side dazzled the viewers with their uniforms. They wore bright red pants, fancy jackets, and white shoe covers. A red Turkish hat with a blue tassel completed the costume. The players put on a good show. The final score was not reported.

TEXT B
Letter From a Soldier

December 26, 1862

Dear Mother,

3   It was hard to be away from home on Christmas. Still, we had a good day. It was like a festival. Firefighters showed off their new fire wagon. Then we had a huge meal. It wasn't your cooking, but it sure tasted good. It was a nice change from our usual meals.

4   The day ended with a baseball game. Some New York regiments set up two teams of nine. I've never seen baseball played before. I know you have not either, so I'll tell you about it. Four bases are set in a large square.

(continued)

At one base, a player with a bat tries to hit a ball thrown by the "pitcher" of the other team. The pitcher's teammates in the field try to catch the hit ball. The batter runs from base to base until he is put out. After three outs, the teams switch places. I sure enjoyed watching the game. Maybe I'll try to get up a team when I return home.

5   A huge crowd showed up to see what baseball was like. Many people who live in the area came, not just us soldiers. They even let the prisoners watch.

Your son,
Abram

1. **What can the reader infer about the writer of Text A?**

   (A) He was a soldier.   (C) He did not like baseball.

   (B) He lived in Hilton Head.   (D) He was not at the game.

2. **Which information is given in Text A but <u>not</u> in Text B?**

   (A) The game took place on Christmas Day.

   (B) Firefighters showed off their new wagon.

   (C) The players were soldiers from New York.

   (D) The game was played in Hilton Head.

3. **Which idea is expressed by the writers of <u>both</u> texts?**

   (A) The team with red pants won the game.

   (B) The food soldiers ate was not very good.

   (C) Baseball was a fairly new sport at that time.

   (D) Baseball uniforms in the 1800s were very colorful.

4. **Which sentence in Text B best shows how the writer feels about baseball? Write the sentence on the lines.**

   _____

   _____

Name: _____ Date: _____

Read both texts about a new bridge. Then answer the questions.

TEXT A

The Opening of the Golden Gate Bridge
(May 27, 1937)

1 **Washington, DC** — The Golden Gate Bridge in San Francisco is finally open! Last Thursday, 200,000 people crossed the bridge on foot. On Friday, more than 32,000 vehicles crossed. A new era in California history has begun.

The Golden Gate Bridge is 1.7 miles long.

2 The city celebrated the opening with a weeklong fiesta and a parade. City leaders made speeches. Bands played. The people chose a Fiesta Queen. Here in Washington, 3,000 miles away, President Roosevelt sent a telegram declaring the bridge open. The United States naval fleet of 42 ships sailed under the bridge. There were more speeches. That night, crowds enjoyed a grand show of fireworks.

3 The idea for a bridge across the Golden Gate Strait goes back to at least 1872. People got serious about it in the 1920s. They made plans and raised funds. Construction began on January 5, 1933. Multiple designers and engineers worked on the project. The design of the bridge changed several times. The curious color choice (orange, not the usual gray or silver) had to be approved. People argued over these questions many times, but none of that matters now. The bridge is finished! It is beautiful, and it's open!

(continued)

TEXT B

Walking Across the New Bridge

4   Thursday was the most exciting day we've had since moving here to San Francisco. Momma, Papa, and I got to walk across the new Golden Gate Bridge!

The bridge's opening day was for people only—no cars allowed.

5   We woke up really early that morning. When we got to the bridge, there was already a huge crowd. I didn't mind. It helped keep me warm. I had my heavy coat on, but the wind was cold. At least it wasn't foggy. I could see all the way to the top of the bridge. It's so tall, and it's bright orange! Later, in the sun, it almost looked like gold.

6   We walked about a mile to the middle of the bridge. Then we stood near the side and looked down. That was scary. We were really high in the air. Watching that rough water and the waves down below made me dizzy.

7   People did some crazy things to celebrate. Some roller-skated. Some walked on stilts. Others ran on the bridge. I even saw a fellow tap-dancing his way across! I think they all wanted the honor of being "the first."

8   Our tickets to see the bridge cost 25 cents each. I don't know what they will use all that money for. But it was worth every penny!

---

1.   **This question has two parts. Answer Part A. Then answer Part B.**

PART A

What can the reader infer about the writer of Text A?

(A) He helped plan the opening celebration.

(B) He watched the opening of the bridge.

(C) He heard about the opening but was not there.

(D) He drove a car or truck across the bridge.

(continued)

Golden Gate Bridge

PART B

Choose the sentence from paragraph 2 that supports the answer to Part A. Underline the sentence.

The city celebrated the opening with a weeklong fiesta and a parade. City leaders made speeches. Bands played. The people chose a Fiesta Queen. Here in Washington, 3,000 miles away, President Roosevelt sent a telegram declaring the bridge open. The United States naval fleet of 42 ships sailed under the bridge. There were more speeches. That night, crowds enjoyed a grand show of fireworks.

2. **Which information is given in Text A but <u>not</u> in Text B?**

   (A) The bridge opened on a Thursday.

   (B) A huge crowd walked across the bridge.

   (C) The bridge was painted orange.

   (D) Thousands of cars crossed the bridge.

3. **Which sentences from Text B best show that the writer of the text was at the opening? Choose <u>two</u> answers.**

   (A) "We woke up really early that morning."

   (B) "I could see all the way to the top of the bridge."

   (C) "It's so tall, and it's bright orange!"

   (D) "Then we stood near the side and looked down."

   (E) "People did some crazy things to celebrate."

4. **Which sentence in Text B best shows how the writer felt about going to see the new bridge? Write the sentence on the lines.**

   _____

   _____

5. **What is the main <u>difference</u> between Text A and Text B?**

   (A) Text A is a news report; Text B is a personal account.

   (B) Text A describes the bridge, but Text B does not.

   (C) Text A says the bridge is in San Francisco; Text B does not.

   (D) Text A describes the crowd, but Text B tells only about the writer.

Name: _____ Date: _____

Read both texts about a pilot. Then answer the questions.

TEXT A

First Lady of the Air

Harriet Quimby,
the first female
American pilot

1   The first airplane flew in 1903. The Wright brothers built and piloted the plane. It stayed in the air for only 12 seconds. It traveled only 120 feet. But that was the beginning.

2   Over the next ten years, airplanes changed fast. Flights lasted longer, and planes got better. In the early years, all of the pilots were men. But that changed in 1911. In May, a woman named Harriet Quimby started taking flying lessons on Long Island, New York. In August, she became the first American woman to earn a pilot license.

3   Quimby began flying in air shows that year. She soon became famous for her daring and skill. Then she had a bold idea. She would fly across the English Channel. That is a body of water between England and France. In those days, a flight across water was risky. If something went wrong, the plane could not land. A man flew across the Channel three years earlier, in 1909. But no woman had done it.

4   On April 16, 1912, Harriet Quimby climbed into her plane in Dover, England. She took off from there, flew across the Channel, and landed in Calais, France. By doing so, she earned a new title. She became "America's First Lady of the Air."

(continued)

TEXT B

Harriet Quimby's Description of Her Flight

5   "It was a cold 5:30 A.M. when my machine got off the ground. The noise of the motor drowned the shouts and cheers of friends below. In a moment I was in the air, climbing steadily in a long circle. I was up 1,500 feet within 30 seconds. From this high point my eyes lit at once on Dover Castle. It was half hidden in a fog bank.

6   "In an instant I was beyond the cliffs and over the channel. Then the thick fog obscured my view. Calais was out of sight. I could not see ahead of me or at all below. There was only one thing for me to do. I had to keep my eyes fixed on the compass.

7   "The distance straight across from Dover to Calais is only 22 miles. I knew that land must be in sight if I could only get below the fog and see it. So I dropped from an altitude of about 2,000 feet until I was half that height. The sunlight struck upon my face. My eyes lit upon the white and sandy shores of France. I felt happy, but could not find Calais.

8   "I flew a short distance inland to locate myself or find a good place on which to alight. It was all tilled land below me. Rather than tear up the farmers' fields, I decided to drop down on the hard and sandy beach. I did so at once, making an easy landing. Then I jumped from my machine and was alone upon the shore. But it was only for a few moments. A crowd of fishermen came rushing from all directions toward me. They were chattering in French, but they knew I had crossed the Channel. They were congratulating themselves that the first woman to cross in an airplane had landed on their fishing beach."

Source: www.eyewitnesstohistory.com/quimby.htm

Informational Texts for Striving Readers: Grade 4 © 2021 by Michael Priestley, Scholastic Inc. • page 42

Harriet Quimby

1. **This question has two parts. Answer Part A. Then answer Part B.**

   PART A

   How does the author of Text A feel about Harriet Quimby?

   (A) He admires her.   (C) He feels sorry for her.

   (B) He does not like her.   (D) He thinks she was selfish.

   PART B

   Which sentence from the passage best supports the answer to Part A?

   (A) "The first airplane flew in 1903."

   (B) "In May, a woman named Harriet Quimby started taking flying lessons on Long Island, New York."

   (C) "Quimby began flying in air shows that year."

   (D) "She soon became famous for her daring and skill."

2. **Which sentence in Text A describes a "first" Harriet Quimby became known for?**

   (A) "But that changed in 1911."

   (B) "In August, she became the first American woman to earn a pilot license."

   (C) "Then she had a bold idea."

   (D) "A man flew across the Channel three years earlier, in 1909."

3. **Which sentence in Text B shows how Quimby felt during the flight?**

   (A) "The noise of the motor drowned the shouts and cheers of friends below."

   (B) "I could not see ahead of me or at all below."

   (C) "I felt happy, but could not find Calais."

   (D) "Then I jumped from my machine and was alone upon the shore."

4. **Who first met Harriet Quimby when she landed in France?**

   _____

Name: _____ Date: _____

A Lone Star

1   The state of Texas has a long, rich history—and a special nickname. It is called the "Lone Star State." Why? To answer that question, we must go back in time.

2   People have lived in Texas for at least 12,000 years. At least nine different Native American tribes settled there. They included the Caddo people, the Apache, and the Wichita. Then, in the 1500s, European explorers began to arrive.

3   The first explorers came from Spain in 1519. They sailed along the coast. Others, such as Cabeza de Vaca, went ashore and explored the land. Early visitors were looking for gold. But they found a land rich in other resources instead. Soon afterward, Spain claimed ownership of the whole area and called it Mexico. Texas was part of it.

4   In the 1830s, American settlers in Texas fought a war against Mexico. Under the leadership of Sam Houston, the Texans won the war. They decided to form their own country. It was called the Republic of Texas. This new country shared a long border with Mexico. Their cultures were closely connected—and still are.

5   Since the beginning, every U.S. flag has held one star for each state. In the early years, the United States had 13 states and the flag had 13 stars. As each state joined the country, a star was added to the flag. When Texas became its own country, it created a new flag. It had one star. Texas became the "Lone Star State." That is still its nickname today.

Texas's state flag features one star.

Texas History

1519	Spanish explorers visit Texas coast
1682	First Spanish settlement near El Paso
1718	Alamo built in San Antonio
1821	Mexico wins freedom from Spain
1823	Americans begin to settle in Texas
1836	Texans win freedom from Mexico
1845	Texas joins United States as the 28th state

A Lone Star

1. **Where was the first Spanish settlement in Texas?**

   _____

2. **Which sentence from the passage tells why Spanish explorers first went to Texas?**

   (A) "Then, in the 1500s, European explorers began to arrive."

   (B) "Others, such as Cabeza de Vaca, went ashore and explored the land."

   (C) "Early visitors were looking for gold."

   (D) "But they found a land rich in other resources instead."

3. **In the 1820s, Texas was part of what country?**

   _____

4. **How did Texans win their freedom in 1836?**

   (A) They built the Alamo.   (C) They joined the United States.

   (B) They settled in Mexico.   (D) They fought a war against Mexico.

5. **Choose two sentences from the last paragraph that explain why Texas is called the "Lone Star State." Underline the sentences.**

   Since the beginning, every U.S. flag has held one star for each state. In the early years, the United States had 13 states and the flag had 13 stars. As each state joined the country, a star was added to the flag. When Texas became its own country, it created a new flag. It had one star. Texas became the "Lone Star State." That is still its nickname today.

Name: _____   Date: _____

A Side of Ant Eggs

1   Visitors from other countries might think that
Americans eat some strange foods. Have you
tried a corn dog or a hamburger served on
a doughnut? How about tater tot casserole?
Or deep-fried butter? Maybe you'd like
to try pickled pigs' feet? All these
are actual American foods. To some
of us, they don't seem that unusual.

A corn dog is a hot dog
on a stick, coated with
batter and deep fried.

2   We may think that some of the foods
people in other countries eat are strange.
But they are just ordinary foods to the people
who eat them all the time. One example is
beondegi (buhn-day-gee). These are silkworm pupae,
or cocoons. In South Korea, this is a popular snack.
Street vendors sell it. They boil or steam the cocoons, then serve
them in a paper cup with a toothpick. People say it tastes kind of nutty.

3   China has many kinds of unusual foods. Snack shops on the street
may serve fried scorpions. These popular snacks are served on a stick.
They taste kind of like potato chips. Other shops may serve crickets and
grasshoppers. Both have plenty of protein.

4   In many countries, people find special foods that grow only in certain
places or at certain times. Those foods become special treats. For example,
in Mexico, some people harvest ant eggs. They can be found only in the
roots of agave plants for two months of the year. Pan-fried with onion and
chili, they are served as a side dish. It is called *escamole*. In the Philippines,
some people eat woodworms dipped in vinegar. These worms can only be
found in dead mangrove trees. In Portugal and Spain, people eat something
called *percebes*. These are small sea creatures in shells. They cling to the
sides of rocks. They can be very hard to find and even harder to gather.
But people say they are delicious.

5   Clearly, people in different places eat different foods. Something that
looks yucky to one person might look tasty to another. But you'll never
know what something tastes like until you try it.

(continued)

(left) *Beondegi*, boiled silkworm cocoons

(above) Fried scorpions on a stick

Eight Unusual Foods

The chart lists eight kinds of food popular in other countries. We don't usually see these foods in the United States.

Food Name	Description	Country
Beondegi	silkworms	South Korea
Escargot	snails	France
Cuy	guinea pig	Peru, Chile
Escamole	ant eggs	Mexico
Odori don	live octopus	Japan
Tarantula	large spider	Cambodia
Durian	smelly fruit	Vietnam, Thailand
Woodworms	worms from trees	Philippines

A Side of Ant Eggs

1. **Which sentence best states the main point of this passage?**

   (A) "Visitors from other countries might think that Americans eat some strange foods."

   (B) "China has many kinds of unusual foods."

   (C) "We don't usually see these foods in the United States."

   (D) "Clearly, people in different places eat different foods."

2. **What kind of food is *beondegi*?**

   _____

3. **According to the chart, where do people eat snails?**

   (A) China   (C) Chile

   (B) France   (D) Mexico

4. **What kind of food is durian?**

   (A) seafood   (C) smelly fruit

   (B) guinea pig   (D) large spider

5. **Which of these foods are special treats found only in certain plants? Choose <u>two</u> answers.**

   (A) ant eggs   (D) woodworms

   (B) tarantulas   (E) fried scorpions

   (C) percebes

6. **What conclusion can be drawn from the information in this passage?**

   (A) Most Americans eat corn dogs.

   (B) People eat many kinds of food.

   (C) Some foods are eaten once a year.

   (D) People in other countries eat yucky food.

Name: _____ Date: _____

Man Overboard!

1 It was a warm July night off the coast. John Aldridge and Anthony Sosinski set out from Montauk, New York, on their fishing boat, the *Anna Mary*. A friend, Mike Migliaccio, went with them. The men planned to empty their lobster traps in the morning. The traps were many miles from shore. Sosinski went to sleep at 9:00 P.M. He asked Aldridge to wake him at 11:30. Together, they would get things ready for the next day.

2 Sometime during the night, Aldridge decided to pump water into the lobster tanks on the boat by himself. There was a heavy cooler in the way. As he tried to pull it aside, the handle snapped. He stumbled backward and fell into the ocean. He screamed for his crewmates as the boat sailed away, but they heard nothing.

3 Aldridge was alone in the water. He knew he had to stay calm. Somebody would come looking for him in the morning. He pulled off his rubber fishing boots and poured out the water. He trapped air in each one by forcing the boots underwater upside-down. Then he held one under each arm. They helped him stay afloat.

4 Back on the boat, Migliaccio woke up at 6:00 A.M. When he couldn't find Aldridge, he woke Sosinski. The two men looked everywhere. Then Sosinski radioed the U.S. Coast Guard. "I lost a crew member overboard," he said. "I'm in shock."

5 The person on the other end of the line asked questions. Was Aldridge wearing a life preserver? No. What time did he go overboard? Nobody knew. The answer would be the key to finding him.

6 At the Coast Guard station, Jason Rodocker typed the weather and water temperature into his computer program, SAROPS. He added information about ocean currents. Then he entered the present location of the boat and the speed it had been moving during the night. The crew guessed that Aldridge fell off about 3:30 A.M. That's about when they would have started the water pump, which Aldridge apparently had turned on. The computer used the information they had to draw a map showing where to look. Coast Guard boats, helicopters, and planes headed out to find Aldridge.

(continued)

7   Meanwhile, Aldridge was still floating in the water. He knew that other lobstermen had traps nearby. Each one was attached by rope to a buoy, like a balloon, floating on the surface. When the sun came up, he found a buoy and held on.

8   The search went on for hours. That afternoon, a helicopter pilot decided to fly one last loop before heading home. Lieutenant Ray Jamros saw something in the water and yelled. There was Aldridge, waving wildly. Rescue swimmer Bob Hovey dropped into the water. He put Aldridge in a rescue basket, which was attached by cable to the helicopter. Then the helicopter lifted both men to safety.

9   Sosinski was still searching by boat when he got a call on the radio. "*Anna Mary*, we have your man. He's alive."

10   It was a thrilling moment. The searchers had almost given up hope. But Aldridge had survived by staying calm and thinking clearly. The rescue team did the rest.

The Coast Guard uses a basket to rescue someone from the ocean.

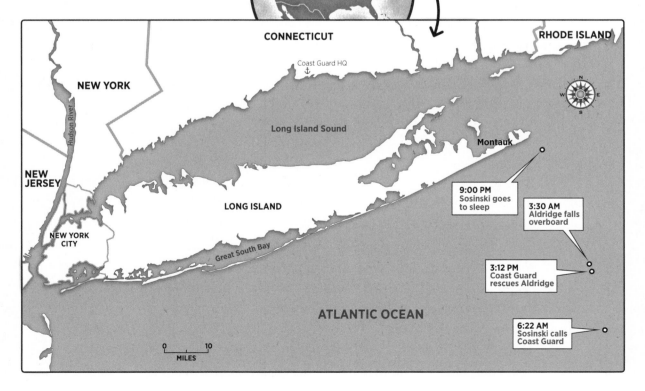

CONNECTICUT

RHODE ISLAND

Coast Guard HQ ⚓

NEW YORK

Long Island Sound

Montauk

NEW JERSEY

LONG ISLAND

NEW YORK CITY

Great South Bay

9:00 PM
Sosinski goes to sleep

3:30 AM
Aldridge falls overboard

3:12 PM
Coast Guard rescues Aldridge

6:22 AM
Sosinski calls Coast Guard

ATLANTIC OCEAN

0   10
MILES

Man Overboard!

1. **Why did John Aldridge and his friends go out on the boat at night?**

   (A) They did not know where their lobster traps were.

   (B) They wanted to get to their lobster traps by morning.

   (C) They had to empty their lobster traps right away.

   (D) They thought other fishermen would take their lobster traps.

2. **Aldridge used his rubber boots to —**

   (A) help him float

   (B) keep his feet warm

   (C) scoop up drinking water

   (D) hold on to a lobster buoy

3. **Based on the map, where did the search take place?**

   _____

4. **Which sentence from paragraph 6 tells how the Coast Guard decided where to search? Write the sentence.**

   _____

   _____

5. **How did the Coast Guard swimmer get Aldridge into the helicopter?**

   (A) He lifted him by his arms.

   (B) He told him to hold on to a buoy.

   (C) He put him in a rescue basket.

   (D) He told the pilot to land on the water.

6. **About how long did Aldridge spend in the water before he was rescued?**

   _____

Name: _____   Date: _____

Discovering Dino-Birds

1   Most scientists today agree that dinosaurs did not all die out.
In fact, they say birds came from dinosaurs.
They developed slowly over a long time.
But scientists didn't always think this.
What changed their minds?

2   New discoveries often change
scientific thinking. In the early 1860s,
a very important fossil was found
in Germany. It had bones and
teeth like a reptile. So it looked
like a dinosaur. But it also had
wings and feathers. Because of those,
the discoverers called it the "first bird."
They named it *Archaeopteryx*, meaning "old wing."

This *Archaeopteryx* fossil
shows imprints of
feathers on the rock.

3   Since then, new kinds of fossils have turned up.
They have convinced scientists that *Archaeopteryx* was more than the
"first bird." It was an important link between birds and dinosaurs.

4   The idea that birds came from dinosaurs really became popular in the
1960s. Fossils of an animal named *Deinonychus* ("terrible claw") provided
a lot of the evidence. This animal had feathers. It was smaller and moved
faster than most dinosaurs. It walked and ran on two legs as birds do.

5   More discoveries have supported scientists' claim. For example, people
have found some dinosaur eggs that are more like bird eggs than reptile
eggs. They have also found male dinosaur fossils beside nests. This
suggests that some male dinosaurs guarded their nests. They also helped
raise their young. Very few reptiles act as parents, but birds do. Some
later fossils show that bones and body structures began to change. They
became lighter and more bird-like. These changes made it possible for the
earliest dino-birds to fly.

6   Scientists continue to find new fossils. New discoveries will add to our
understanding of the connection between birds and dinosaurs.

Discovering Dino-Birds

1. **What made scientists first think that birds came from dinosaurs?**

   (A) digging up eggs   (C) discovering dinosaur nests

   (B) finding *Archaeopteryx*   (D) looking at old fossils in new ways

2. **Which sentence from paragraph 2 tells how *Archaeopteryx* was like a bird? Write the sentence.**

   _____

   _____

3. **Which <u>two</u> sentences from paragraph 4 show how *Deinonychus* was like a bird? Underline the sentences.**

   The idea that birds came from dinosaurs really became popular in the 1960s. Fossils of an animal named *Deinonychus* ("terrible claw") provided a lot of the evidence. This animal had feathers. It was smaller and moved faster than most dinosaurs. It walked and ran on two legs as birds do.

4. **Which sentence from paragraph 5 tells why scientists think that some dinosaurs took care of their young?**

   (A) "For example, people have found some dinosaur eggs that are more like bird eggs than reptile eggs."

   (B) "They have also found male dinosaur fossils beside nests."

   (C) "Very few reptiles act as parents, but birds do."

   (D) "Some later fossils show that bones and body structures began to change."

Name: _____ Date: _____

Getting From Here to There

1   Imagine how different our lives would be without highways. Local streets would be jammed with cars and trucks. Getting anywhere would take a lot longer. You could not get many foods you like because most foods come by truck. Foods from places far away would spoil before reaching your stores. Things you buy online could take weeks for delivery. Family road trips would become harder. By the time you got to where you were going, it would be time to go home!

2   A strong nation needs good highways. It needs high-speed roads connecting cities all across the country. It needs bridges to cross rivers. And it must keep those roads and bridges in good condition. Today, we have a great highway system in the United States. But it wasn't always that way.

3   In the 1950s, President Eisenhower pushed hard for a national highway system. His main concern was safety. He worried that the country might face a war or other emergency. Without highways, moving supplies and troops around would take too long. Eisenhower knew what he was talking about. In 1919, he took part in a test conducted by the Army. He and others drove 81 vehicles from the East Coast to the West. The roads were terrible. The vehicles kept getting stuck. They sometimes had to go far out of the way to find a bridge. The trip took 62 days. Today, it would take only about four.

4   Building a highway system wasn't easy. People argued about what cities to connect. They argued about who should be in charge. They argued about who would repair the roads and bridges after they were built. Above all, they argued about who would pay for everything. In the end, though, they found ways to agree.

5   The government passed the Highway Act in 1956. Work on the highways began soon after that. The last one was completed in 1992, in Colorado. Engineers started with a map of the United States, which had 48 states at the time. They planned to lay out nine interstate highways connecting the East and West coasts. These routes were numbered with even numbers: 10, 20, 30, and so on. Then they laid out major roads going north and south.

(continued)

Informational Texts for Striving Readers: Grade 4 © 2021 by Michael Priestley, Scholastic Inc. • page 54

These routes got odd numbers: 5, 15, 25, and so on. All of these highways were designed to connect major cities. Building all of them took almost 40 years.

6   The National Highway System changed life in America. Different parts of the country became connected. Both people and products could move quickly to all parts of the country. Trucks could carry goods from one place to another. People could more easily visit other regions. It gave new meaning to the name "United States."

Route numbers on highway signs help travelers know where they are going.

1.   **What evidence does the author provide to support the idea that life without highways would be very different? Choose <u>two</u> answers.**

(A) Going anyplace by car would take a lot longer.

(B) People could not visit different parts of the country.

(C) Many farm products would never make it to stores.

(D) Cars would take four days to travel across the country.

(E) There would be few bridges big enough for cars and trucks.

2.   **This question has two parts. Answer Part A. Then answer Part B.**

PART A
Why did President Eisenhower want a national highway system?

(A) to help pay for new roads and bridges

(B) to prevent an attack on the United States

(C) to make it easier to take action in an emergency

(D) to encourage people to drive from one coast to the other

(continued)

Getting From Here to There

PART B

Which sentence in paragraph 3 best supports the answer to Part A? Underline the sentence.

In the 1950s, President Eisenhower pushed hard for a national highway system. His main concern was safety. He worried that the country might face a war or other emergency. Without highways, moving supplies and troops around would take too long. Eisenhower knew what he was talking about. In 1919, he took part in a test conducted by the Army. He and others drove 81 vehicles from the East Coast to the West. The roads were terrible. The vehicles kept getting stuck. They sometimes had to go far out of the way to find a bridge. The trip took 62 days. Today, it would take only about four.

3. **Why did it take so long to drive across the country in 1919? Choose <u>two</u> answers.**

    (A) There were not enough bridges.

    (B) It was hard to find food for everyone.

    (C) There were no fuel stations near the roads.

    (D) Bad roads caused cars and trucks to get stuck.

    (E) Vehicles in those days had to stop more often.

4. **Which sentence from the passage best supports the claim that building the highway system wasn't easy?**

    (A) "A strong nation needs good highways."

    (B) "In the 1950s, President Eisenhower pushed hard for a national highway system."

    (C) "People argued about what cities to connect."

    (D) "In the end, though, they found ways to agree."

5. **The passage claims that Eisenhower's highway system helped unite the country. Write <u>two</u> sentences from the passage that support this claim.**

    _____

    _____

Name: _____ Date: _____

Learning From Home

1   Sometimes students can't go to school in the usual way. They might be sick or live too far away. Something might happen to the school building or the roads so they can't go in. Or some disaster, such as a global pandemic, might force most people to stay home. That's what happened in 2020. In such cases, distance learning can help. It lets students keep up with their studies wherever they are.

What is distance learning?

2   Distance learning means the teacher and students are in different places. Sometimes those places are quite far from each other. That's why distance learning is also called "remote learning." *Remote* means "far away."

3   What we call distance learning is not the same as online learning. Online learning is doing schoolwork on the internet. Teachers may use it in a regular classroom. Or there may be no teacher at all—just a student working on lessons alone. With distance learning, there is always a teacher.

4   Distance learning is not new. For example, Alaska has had students in remote areas doing schoolwork by mail since the 1930s. (In some cases, their lessons and books were delivered by airplane!) Later, radio allowed them to talk with far-off teachers. Today, technology allows students and teachers to join "classrooms" on the internet and connect in many other ways.

What's so good about distance learning?

5   When regular schooling gets interrupted, distance learning keeps students and teachers connected. Teachers can help students when they need it, as in a regular classroom. Students can share ideas. They can have group discussions. Everyone can see how everyone else is doing. This is important for learning. It also makes students happier than studying alone.

6   Distance learning can also take students beyond their own school and community. Experts can "visit" the classroom. Guides can lead "field trips" anywhere in the world. With the right technology, students can study ocean life, explore a tomb in Egypt, or even travel into space.

(continued)

It's not perfect.

7   To be effective, distance learning needs technology. But not every student has a computer or access to one. Not every family has internet service. Some internet connections may be weak or break down a lot.

Distance learning requires a computer or mobile device and an internet connection.

8   Also, distance learning does not work well for every subject. For example, music teachers can show how to hold a certain instrument. But they cannot move students' hands to the right position.

9   Finally, distance learning does not work well for everyone. Some students—and teachers, too—just perform better with other people around. But with time and effort, it can work. Besides, sometimes it may be the only way for students to go to school.

---

1. **Which <u>three</u> sentences in paragraph 1 tell why students might need to learn from home? Underline the sentences.**

    Sometimes students can't go to school in the usual way. They might be sick or live too far away. Something might happen to the school building or the roads so they can't go in. Or some disaster, such as a global pandemic, might force most people to stay home. That's what happened in 2020. In such cases, distance learning can help. It lets students keep up with their studies wherever they are.

2. **Which sentence supports the claim that distance learning is not new?**

  (A) "Distance learning means the teacher and students are in different places."

  (B) "What we call distance learning is not the same as online learning."

  (C) "For example, Alaska has had students in remote areas doing schoolwork by mail since the 1930s."

  (D) "Today, technology allows students and teachers to join 'classrooms' on the internet and connect in many other ways."

(continued)

Learning From Home

3. **This question has two parts. Answer Part A. Then answer Part B.**

   PART A

   How does the author describe distance learning?

   (A) It should be used only in cases of emergency.

   (B) It helps students in more ways than just learning.

   (C) It is the best kind of education for most students.

   (D) It makes schoolwork much harder for most students.

   PART B

   Which sentence best supports the answer to Part A?

   (A) "When regular schooling gets interrupted, distance learning keeps students and teachers connected."

   (B) "Teachers can help students when they need it, as in a regular classroom."

   (C) "They can have group discussions."

   (D) "It also makes students happier than studying alone."

4. **Distance learning depends on technology. Which two sentences tell why this is sometimes a problem?**

   (A) "Experts can 'visit' the classroom."

   (B) "With the right technology, students can study ocean life, explore a tomb in Egypt, or even travel into space."

   (C) "But not every student has a computer or access to one."

   (D) "Some internet connections may be weak or break down a lot."

   (E) "Also, distance learning does not work well for every subject."

5. **According to the author, distance learning is good for students because they can —**

   (A) become comfortable with technology

   (B) work on their lessons when they feel ready

   (C) choose teachers they feel comfortable with

   (D) experience the world beyond their own community

Name: _____   Date: _____

A Funny Guy

Dav Pilkey

1   Dav Pilkey is an author and illustrator of children's books. He is best known for his picture books, chapter books, and graphic novels. They tell stories through pictures, cartoons, and words. His most popular series are Dog Man and Captain Underpants.

2   When Dav was young, he struggled in school. He was diagnosed with ADHD and dyslexia. It was hard for him to sit still. He acted out in class. As a result, his teachers often made him sit in the hall. To pass the time, Dav drew comics and wrote adventure stories. He made up his own characters, including Dog Man and Captain Underpants. Dav's classmates thought his stories were funny. But his teachers did not agree.

3   Through high school and college, Pilkey continued to draw comics and make up stories. One of his professors thought he was very talented. She encouraged him to write a book for children. So he did. His first book, *World War Won*, was published in 1987.

4   A lot of the characters in Pilkey's books come from the comics he had made as a kid. For example, George and Harold, the two main characters from the Captain Underpants series, are based on his own life. Like him, the boys enjoy making silly comics. They sometimes have trouble behaving in school, too.

5   The Captain Underpants series has been made into a movie and TV series. Dog Man has been made into a musical. Pilkey's latest graphic novel series is Cat Kid Comic Club. Kids around the world love his books.

Dog Man

Dog Man is Pilkey's favorite character. He thought of the idea for the character in second grade. In his childhood stories, Dog Man often got struck by lightning. The lightning gave Dog Man superpowers, which he used to save the day. Pilkey changed the character for the books he writes today. In the Dog Man graphic novels, Dog Man is part dog and part man. But of course, he still always saves the day. Pilkey says Dog Man is both lovable and loyal—two things he loves about real dogs.

A Funny Guy

1. **How are the characters in Dog Man and Captain Underpants alike?**

   (A) They often save people.

   (B) They get into trouble in school.

   (C) Pilkey's teachers liked them.

   (D) Pilkey made them up when he was a kid.

2. **How are his characters George and Harold like Dav Pilkey? Choose <u>two</u> answers.**

   (A) They like dogs.

   (B) They go to college.

   (C) They like to make comics.

   (D) They have trouble behaving in school.

   (E) They want to be captains.

3. **Decide whether each sentence describes the Dog Man books, the Captain Underpants books, or both. Check the correct box beside each sentence.**

	Dog Man	Captain Underpants	Both
It has silly characters.			
Its main character has superpowers.			
It is a graphic novel.			
It was made into a movie.			

4. **What information is found in the sidebar that is <u>not</u> in the passage?**

   (A) Dog Man is Pilkey's favorite character.

   (B) Pilkey drew cartoons when he was a child.

   (C) Pilkey had trouble learning when he was young.

   (D) Dog Man is one of Pilkey's most popular series.

Name: _____ Date: _____

The Great Barrier Reef

A diver observes some of the fish that live in the Great Barrier Reef.

1   Do you know what the world's largest living structure is? It's the Great Barrier Reef (GBR)! This colorful coral reef sits in the Pacific Ocean near the coast of Australia. It is more than 1,400 miles long. It is so large that it can be seen from space.

2   Coral reefs look like plants, but they are actually hard skeletons. They are made by tiny animals called *polyps*. The polyps eat *algae*, which are plants. Then they produce waste, which hardens into coral. The coral reef gets its pretty colors from the algae.

3   Polyps are very delicate. If the ocean temperature rises just a little bit, it can hurt the polyps. The polyps become stressed and turn white. This is called *bleaching*. If the water temperature returns to normal, the polyps can get their color back. But the polyps can die if they are white for too long.

4   The GBR had a major bleaching event in 2016. Australia was very hot that summer. The heat wave made the ocean temperatures rise, and many coral reefs turned white. Luckily, some of them recovered, but experts are worried. Global temperatures have been rising every year, and this will warm the oceans. That means more bleaching events are likely.

(continued)

5   The GBR supports a huge amount of plant and animal life. In fact, it is home to more than 1,500 species of fish. Thirty types of whales and dolphins live there, as do 215 types of birds. There are also 400 different kinds of coral.

6   The GBR draws about 2 million tourists every year. People like to dive and snorkel by the reef. They want to see the tropical fish and colorful coral. But diving can cause problems for the reef. If a diver touches or kicks the reef, the reef can break apart. Divers need to be very careful. A program called Green Fins is designed to help. It teaches people how to dive safely. It also shows them how to act around coral reefs.

7   The Great Barrier Reef is a natural wonder. We need to keep it safe.

Threats to Coral Reefs

Pollution. Run-off from city streets and farms ends up in the ocean. The run-off may contain anything from soap to weed-killer to paint. These things harm the polyps. They also make the water murky so the sun can't shine through. Polyps need sunlight to live.

Climate Change. Temperatures around the globe are rising, and oceans are getting warmer. Coral reefs become stressed in water that is too warm. This leads to bleaching, which can cause them to die.

Human Interactions. Divers may bump into the coral reefs and break them. Divers should never touch the corals. They should not pollute the water or leave trash behind either.

1. **Why is the Great Barrier Reef important?**

   (A) It is very beautiful.

   (B) It is a nice place to visit.

   (C) It can be seen from space.

   (D) It is home to many kinds of animals.

2. **What <u>two</u> pieces of information does the sidebar add to the passage?**

   (A) Algae are tiny plants.

   (B) Run-off from farms can harm coral reefs.

   (C) Coral gets its colors from algae.

   (D) The Great Barrier Reef is more than 1,400 miles long.

   (E) Polyps need sunlight to live.

   (continued)

The Great Barrier Reef

3. **What causes the bleaching of coral reefs?**

_____

_____

_____

4. **Decide whether each piece of information in the chart is found in the passage, the sidebar, or both. Check the correct box beside each one.**

	Passage	Sidebar	Both
Healthy coral reefs are colorful.			
Over 400 types of coral live in the Great Barrier Reef.			
Pollution from cities and farms can harm coral reefs.			
Divers can damage the Great Barrier Reef.			
The Green Fins program teaches people how to dive near coral reefs.			

5. **What information is given in the passage but <u>not</u> in the sidebar?**

A Scuba divers can damage coral reefs.

B Climate change is harming coral reefs.

C Two million people visit the reef each year.

D Coral reefs need sunlight to stay healthy.

Name: _____   Date: _____

Machu Picchu

1   High in the Andes Mountains in Peru, an amazing stone city sits. It is called Machu Picchu (MAH-chu PEEK-chu). The Inca people built it in the 1400s. But then it sat empty for hundreds of years.

Machu Picchu spreads out over five miles.

2   Peru is a country in South America. During the 1100s, the Inca people settled there. They built Machu Picchu on the side of a hill. They built terraces with stone steps that link each level. In fact, there are more than 3,000 steps in Machu Picchu! The site has nearly 200 stone buildings. They include houses, temples, storerooms, and baths. They had roofs made of dried grasses called *thatch*.

3   Building such a city so long ago was not an easy feat. Some of the stones weighed many tons. No one is sure how people moved and lifted the stones.

4   Historians believe Machu Picchu was used for only about 100 years. It may have been a summer home for the emperor. Or it may have been a place for the Inca to hide from their enemies. When Spanish invaders took over the area around 1572, the Inca left Machu Picchu.

5   Today, Machu Picchu is a popular place to visit. But historians want to protect it. Too many visitors will damage the ruins.

Hiram Bingham's Discovery

Hiram Bingham was an American explorer. In 1911, he set out to find a "lost city" in the Andes he had heard about.

Bingham and his team met a local farmer in Peru. The farmer told them about ruins on top of a mountain. The man called it Machu Picchu, which means "old mountain." Bingham was eager to find this lost city.

The next day his team climbed up the mountain. They met an 11-year-old boy, who showed them the way to the ruins. Bingham was amazed at the stone city before him.

Bingham wrote a book about his discovery. Today, more than a million people visit Machu Picchu every year.

Machu Picchu

1. **Which detail from the passage tells what Machu Picchu looked like?**

   (A) "The Inca people built it in the 1400s."

   (B) "During the 1100s, the Inca people settled there."

   (C) "They built terraces with stone steps that link each level."

   (D) "Building such a city so long ago was not an easy feat."

2. **Who built Machu Picchu?**

   _____

3. **What <u>two</u> pieces of information does the sidebar add to the passage?**

   (A) Many people visit Machu Picchu.

   (B) The name Machu Picchu means "old mountain."

   (C) Machu Picchu is in the Andes Mountains.

   (D) Wealthy Inca people lived in Machu Picchu.

   (E) Hiram Bingham found Machu Picchu in 1911.

4. **Which sentence from the passage tells why Machu Picchu was called a "lost city"?**

   (A) "They built Machu Picchu on the side of a hill."

   (B) "But then it sat empty for hundreds of years."

   (C) "Some of the stones weighed many tons."

   (D) "Today, Machu Picchu is a popular place to visit."

5. **According to the passage, what was Machu Picchu built for? Give <u>two</u> reasons.**

   _____

   _____

   _____

Name: _____ Date: _____

Strong and Honest Abe

1   People remember Abraham Lincoln as the 16th President of the United States. But did you know that he was also a star wrestler? Historians say that young Abe fought 300 matches and lost only one.

2   At 6 feet 4 inches tall, Lincoln towered over most of his opponents. He was also very strong and very smart. Sometimes he won matches just by being clever or by teasing his opponents.

3   In one match, his strength, skill, and wit were not enough. He lost to Lorenzo Dow Thompson in 1832. Lincoln said the match was "the fiercest struggle of the like that I ever had." Lincoln's friends watched the fight. They said nobody won or lost. But Lincoln disagreed. He said that Thompson won fair and square. Lincoln accepted defeat, adding, "Why, gentlemen, that man could throw a grizzly bear."

1. What is the main idea of this passage?

(A) Lincoln was smarter than his opponents.

(B) Abe Lincoln was taller than most men.

(C) Abraham Lincoln was the 16th president.

(D) President Lincoln was a good wrestler.

2. Which sentence from the passage shows that Lincoln was an honest man? Write the sentence.

_____

_____

3. What did Lincoln mean when he said that Thompson "could throw a grizzly bear"?

(A) Thompson fought like a wild animal.

(B) Thompson usually fought with bears.

(C) Thompson was a very strong wrestler.

(D) Thompson liked to throw heavy objects.

Name: _____ Date: _____

Who Needs Bees?

1   We know that bees make honey and they sometimes sting. But bees do more than that. Without them, many of our foods would disappear. Bees are natural *pollinators*. They carry pollen from plant to plant. The pollen helps the plants make the fruits, vegetables, and grains we eat.

As a bee feeds on a flower, pollen sticks to its body. The bee carries the pollen to other flowers.

2   Bees need our help. Poisons, plant diseases, changing climate, and other threats are killing our bees. Without bees, many plants will not grow. With a little work, you can help save the bees by planting a garden. You will be helping butterflies, birds, and bats, too.

How to Plant a Pollinator Garden

1. Choose a sunny spot outdoors. It doesn't have to be large—even one flowering plant hanging from a post will help.

2. Decide what kinds of plants you want to grow. Flowers with interesting smells and bright colors attract more bees. Flowers with large single blooms provide more nectar, which is what bees eat. Different plants bloom at different times of the year. If you have plants that "take turns," you'll always have something the bees like.

3. Buy some seeds or a few young plants, and start your plants in pots or in the soil outdoors. Make sure they'll get plenty of sun.

4. Water the plants when the soil gets dry.

5. Remember that bees need to drink. Fill a shallow bowl with water, and add a few stones, twigs, or floating corks for visitors to land on. Clean the container and change the water every couple of days.

6. If you see birds, bees, or other flying insects on your plants, they are doing their job—and your garden is helping.

(continued)

Informational Texts for Striving Readers: Grade 4 © 2021 by Michael Priestley, Scholastic Inc. • page 68

3   Scientists estimate that for every three bites of food we eat, one of them depends on pollinators. Next time you swat a bee away from your picnic, remember that without these insects, we might not have food for picnics at all.

---

1. How do bees help food grow?

(A) They carry pollen from plant to plant.

(B) They use nectar from flowers to make honey.

(C) They carry seeds from one place to another.

(D) They visit plants with interesting smells and bright colors.

2. Which sentence in the passage tells why bees need our help? Write the sentence.

_____

_____

3. What is most important in deciding which plants to grow in a pollinator garden?

(A) Plant flowers that are all the same color.

(B) Choose flowers that bees like.

(C) Find plants of different heights.

(D) Make sure the flowers are large.

4. Besides flowering plants, what else should be in a pollinator garden?

(A) stones   (C) twigs

(B) bowls   (D) water

Name: _____ Date: _____

Ancient Fish in Danger

Sturgeons can live more than 100 years. They can weigh as much as 800 pounds and grow to 14 feet long.

1   Dinosaurs weren't the only animals that lived millions of years ago. Other creatures also inhabited the Earth. But then a huge asteroid struck our planet. Dirt and dust from the explosion filled the air, causing a long period of cold and darkness. Green plants died, so animals could not find food. Most of the dinosaurs died out, but some fish and birds survived. One of them was a large fish called a *sturgeon* (STIR-jin).

2   Most sturgeons live in rivers and lakes. They are bottom-feeders. They eat worms, mussels, and other things that live in the sand and mud. Even when rivers and lakes freeze, sturgeons can find food. In this way, they have survived millions of years.

3   The past 100 years have brought a new challenge for these fish. People around the world like to eat the eggs of some fish. These eggs are called *caviar*. The most popular kind of caviar is sturgeon eggs. Since people ate millions of tiny sturgeon eggs, these eggs did not hatch and few sturgeon babies were born.

4   By the 1990s, sturgeons were almost wiped out. New laws stopped overfishing and reduced the amount of caviar that people could take and sell as food. Efforts like these helped sturgeon populations grow again, but full recovery will take a long time. These ancient fish have been around millions of years. Let's make sure they continue to survive.

Ancient Fish in Danger

1. **What is the main idea of this passage?**

   (A) Dinosaurs lived on Earth a long time ago.

   (B) A sturgeon can grow to 800 pounds and 14 feet long.

   (C) Sturgeons have survived for millions of years.

   (D) Scientists think that a large asteroid struck Earth.

2. **Which sentences describe the effects of an asteroid hitting Earth long ago? Choose <u>two</u> answers.**

   (A) "Dinosaurs weren't the only animals that lived millions of years ago."

   (B) "Dirt and dust from the explosion filled the air, causing a long period of cold and darkness."

   (C) "Green plants died, so animals could not find food."

   (D) "One of them was a large fish called a *sturgeon*."

   (E) "Most sturgeons live in rivers and lakes."

3. **What do sturgeons eat?**

   _____

4. **Which sentence from the passage best explains why sturgeons were almost wiped out by the 1990s?**

   (A) "Most of the dinosaurs died out, but some fish and birds survived."

   (B) "The past 100 years have brought a new challenge for these fish."

   (C) "People around the world like to eat the eggs of some fish."

   (D) "Since people ate millions of tiny sturgeon eggs, these eggs did not hatch and few sturgeon babies were born."

Practice Test

Name: _____ Date: _____

Read each passage and answer the questions that follow.

PASSAGE A
Help From the Ocean

1   More than 70 percent of our world is covered with ocean. It is home to many living things. Ocean animals and plants are helpful to humans in many ways. Here are a few examples.

2   **A Sea Animal That Teaches** The sea lamprey looks like a snake or an eel. It also has an unusual ability. Its *spinal cord*, the big nerve that runs the length of its body, can grow back if it gets cut. Before long, the lamprey can swim just as well as it did before. When nerves in the human body are damaged, they do not grow back. So lampreys can teach scientists about how nerves can recover. Maybe someday, scientists will learn how to help people's nerves grow back, just like the lamprey's.

Sea lamprey

3   **A Plant That Gels** A substance in seaweed is used to make many products. It is called *carrageenan*. It comes from red seaweed. A very small amount of it can turn a liquid into a gel. So it is used to make certain foods, such as pudding, jam, and ice cream. It is also used to make shampoo, toothpaste, and paint. Next time you brush your teeth, you may be brushing with seaweed!

4   **Turning Scales Into Plastic** Humans **produce** a lot of plastic. Most of it is made from *petroleum*, or oil. An English scientist named Lucy Hughes learned that the fishing industry creates a lot of waste. She wanted to find a way to use that waste. So she invented a plastic that is made from fish scales. She called it "MarinaTex." This plastic is clear, flexible, and very strong. It can be used to make plastic bags and wrapping for food products. Most of the plastics we now throw away will stay around for hundreds of years. That will cause some huge problems in the future. But this new plastic breaks down in only four to six weeks. Once again, the sea may help us solve a challenging problem.

PASSAGE A: Help From the Ocean

1. **This question has two parts. Answer Part A. Then answer Part B.**

   PART A
   What is the main idea of this passage?

   (A) People use a lot of plastic.

   (B) The world's oceans are enormous.

   (C) Ocean animals and plants can help people.

   (D) Many plants and animals live in the oceans.

   PART B
   Which sentence from paragraph 2 best supports the main idea?

   (A) "The sea lamprey looks like a snake or an eel."

   (B) "Before long, the lamprey can swim just as well as it did before."

   (C) "When nerves in the human body are damaged, they do not grow back."

   (D) "So lampreys can teach scientists about how nerves can recover."

2. **Name two things that are made with a substance from red seaweed.**

   _____

   _____

3. **What is the meaning of the word _produce_ in the last paragraph?**

   (A) make   (C) need

   (B) sell   (D) destroy

4. **Which sentence from the last paragraph tells why Lucy Hughes invented a new plastic?**

   (A) "Most of it is made from _petroleum_, or oil."

   (B) "She wanted to find a way to use that waste."

   (C) "This plastic is clear, flexible, and very strong."

   (D) "But this new plastic breaks down in only four to six weeks."

5. **What text structure does the author use in most of this passage?**

   (A) time order   (C) cause and effect

   (B) comparison and contrast   (D) problem and solution

PASSAGE B

Living a Dream

1   Jessica Meir grew up in a small city called Caribou. It is in northern Maine. When she looked up at the stars, she dreamed of being an astronaut. She probably never imagined that she would live more than six months in space.

2   The International Space Station, or ISS, is a giant space lab. It has flown around Earth for more than 20 years. The ISS is shared by five space agencies: the United States, Russia, Japan, Europe, and Canada. Astronauts from several countries live and work on the space station for months at a time. They learn about space and do science experiments.

Before she became an astronaut, Jessica Meir was both a pilot and an aquanaut. An aquanaut is a scientist who works underwater.

3   From September 2019 through April 2020, Jessica Meir lived on the ISS. One of her crewmates came from Russia. On October 18, 2019, Meir and her other crewmate, Christina Koch, made history. They did the first all-woman spacewalk. They walked in space three different times. In total, they spent about 22 hours outside the space station.

4   During her time on ISS, Meir spent 205 days in space. She traveled 86.9 million miles. She orbited Earth 3,280 times. She remembers the night sky from her childhood in Maine. Looking up at that sky made her want to travel into space—and she did.

PASSAGE B: Living a Dream

6. **What made Jessica Meir want to become an astronaut?**

    (A) living in Maine   (C) becoming a pilot

    (B) walking in space   (D) looking at the stars

7. **Which sentence from the passage shows that Meir did something no one had ever done before?**

    (A) "She probably never imagined that she would live more than six months in space."

    (B) "From September 2019 through April 2020, Jessica Meir lived on the ISS."

    (C) "They did the first all-woman spacewalk."

    (D) "During her time on ISS, Meir spent 205 days in space."

8. **What can the reader learn about the ISS from this passage? Choose <u>two</u> answers.**

    (A) It has many connected parts.

    (B) It is shared by several countries.

    (C) It circles Earth every 92 minutes.

    (D) It carries astronauts to the moon.

    (E) It has flown for more than 20 years.

9. **According to the photo caption, what did Jessica Meir do <u>before</u> she went into space?**

    _____

10. **What is the author's view of Jessica Meir?**

    (A) She admires her.   (C) She is proud of her.

    (B) She dislikes her.   (D) She envies her.

Informational Texts for Striving Readers: Grade 4 © 2021 by Michael Priestley, Scholastic Inc. • page 76

PASSAGE C

Back to the Moon

1   The United States plans to send astronauts back to the moon. How will they get there? They will ride on *Orion*, a new spacecraft that is part of a NASA program called "Artemis."

2   NASA's space programs began about 60 years ago. The Mercury program was the first to send astronauts into space. It began in 1961. The first flight lasted only 15 minutes. Next was the Gemini program. It began in 1965. Flights into space got longer. The first walk in space took place, and two spacecraft docked with each other. The Apollo program began in 1968. It led to six moon landings.

3   After that came the Space Shuttles. The shuttle was the first spacecraft that could go into space, return to Earth, and be used again. Shuttles flew from 1981 to 2011. Astronauts rode on the shuttles to build the International Space Station (ISS), beginning in 1998. Fifteen countries worked together to build it. The ISS travels around Earth. It has room for as many as ten people to live on board.

4   After NASA ended the shuttle program, the U.S. had no way to send astronauts into space. Astronauts going to the ISS had to get a ride on Russia's shuttle instead.

5   But now, NASA has new goals and a new spacecraft: *Orion*. It will carry four astronauts and everything they will need to live in space for weeks at a time. NASA wants to return to the moon and build a station there by 2028. NASA also plans to build a spaceport called *Gateway*, which will circle the moon. It will serve as a place for astronauts to prepare before missions to the moon. Someday, it will help astronauts go to Mars.

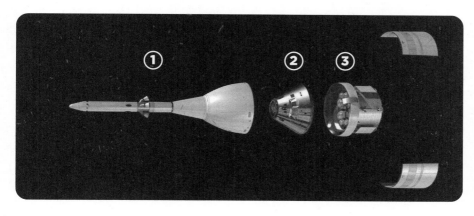

Orion has three parts:

1. a safety system

2. the crew module, where astronauts will live and work

3. the service module

PASSAGE C: Back to the Moon

11. **What is the main idea of this passage?**

   (A) The first U.S. astronauts went into space in 1961.

   (B) The U.S. has a long history of space exploration.

   (C) Space shuttles were used to build the space station.

   (D) NASA plans to explore the moon and then go to Mars.

12. **What text structure does the author use to present most of the information in this passage?**

   (A) time order

   (B) cause and effect

   (C) problem and solution

   (D) comparison and contrast

13. **Based on the picture, which part of the *Orion* spacecraft will astronauts ride in?**

   _____

The next two questions are about both Passages B and C.

14. **Which detail appears in <u>both</u> Passage B and Passage C?**

   (A) Fifteen countries helped build the ISS.

   (B) The first U.S. space flight was in 1961.

   (C) Astronauts live and work on the ISS.

   (D) Someday people will travel to Mars.

15. **Read the detail sentences below. Decide whether each detail appears in Passage B, Passage C, or both. Check the correct box beside each sentence.**

Details	Passage B	Passage C	Both
In the Apollo program, people landed on the moon.			
Two women walked in space in 2019.			
The ISS travels around Earth.			
The U.S. shares the ISS with other countries.			
NASA plans to return to the moon.			

PASSAGE D
The Bull-Dogger

1   Born in Texas around 1870, Bill Pickett was the second of 13 children. His family was of Black and Cherokee heritage. As a boy, Bill learned to ride horses and rope cattle. As a teenager, he worked on a ranch. Bill was a good worker, but he was a great performer. He did tricks in local rodeos. The crowds loved him. He and his brother started the Pickett Brothers Bronco Busters and Rough Riders Show. They **toured** county fairs all over Texas and Oklahoma.

In 1971, Bill Pickett became the first Black American to be named to the National Cowboy Hall of Fame.

2   In 1907, Pickett joined the 101 Ranch Wild West Show. For the show he invented a trick called *bull-dogging*. This meant jumping from a moving horse, grabbing a bull around the neck or by the horns, and pulling it to the ground. It was dangerous, but it was fun to watch. And it did not hurt the bull. Bill Pickett soon became the star of the show. In 1908, he wrestled a bull in Mexico City for seven minutes!

3   Pickett performed in rodeo shows for more than 30 years. He even traveled to England to perform. Then, in 1921, he got a chance to do something special. He acted in a movie about himself. It was called *The Bull-Dogger*. It told about how he grew up and showed him doing his best tricks. Sadly, the film has been lost. Luckily, the story of Bill Pickett has not.

PASSAGE D: The Bull-Dogger

16. **What is the meaning of the word *toured* in the first paragraph?**

(A) started

(B) followed

(C) worked at

(D) traveled to

17. **What did Bill Pickett become famous for?**

(A) riding horses

(B) wrestling bulls

(C) training dogs

(D) acting in movies

18. **Which sentence in the first paragraph shows how people felt about Bill Pickett? Underline the sentence.**

Born in Texas around 1870, Bill Pickett was the second of 13 children. His family was of Black and Cherokee heritage. As a boy, he learned to ride horses and rope cattle. As a teenager, he worked on a ranch. Bill was a good worker, but he was a great performer. He did tricks in local rodeos. The crowds loved him. He and his brother started the Pickett Brothers Bronco Busters and Rough Riders Show. They toured county fairs all over Texas and Oklahoma.

19. **Which sentence from the passage tells why people enjoyed "bull-dogging"?**

(A) "For the show he invented a trick called *bull-dogging*."

(B) "This meant jumping from a moving horse, grabbing the bull around the neck or by the horns, and pulling it to the ground."

(C) "It was dangerous, but it was fun to watch."

(D) "Bill Pickett soon became the star of the show."

20. **What honor was given to Bill Pickett in 1971?**

_____

_____

PASSAGE E
City of the Rising Sun

1   Every morning, people on the eastern shores of Japan can watch the sun rise over the Pacific Ocean. So this Asian country became known as the "Land of the Rising Sun." Japan has four main islands and hundreds of smaller ones.

2   Centuries ago, on the main island of Honshu, people settled in a fishing village called Edo. Edo grew into a city, which got larger and larger. In 1868, it became the capital of Japan. Its name was changed to Tokyo. Today, greater Tokyo is the largest city in the whole world. More than 38 million people live there.

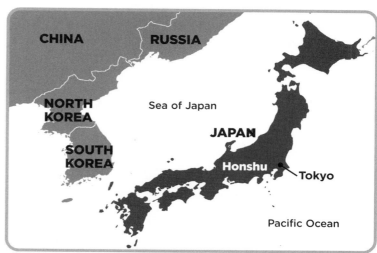

Japan is surrounded by the Pacific Ocean and the Sea of Japan.

3   For Japan, Tokyo is the center of government, business, and culture. It has many schools, stores, parks, and museums. It is the **hub** of the country. Railroads, bus lines, and highways all come together in Tokyo. It has two busy airports.

4   In the center of the city sits the Imperial Palace. This is the home of the Emperor of Japan and his family. Japan's government makes laws and rules the country. But the Emperor is the honored leader, like a king or queen. Every year, on January 2, the Emperor welcomes visitors to his home. He gives a short speech to wish everyone good health and good luck.

5   There is so much to do in Tokyo. The city has many gardens and temples. You can eat sushi (raw fish) and go to noodle shops. You can go to special theaters to see plays. You can watch sumo wrestling and baseball games. You can see the Olympic park built in 2020. You can also visit some very tall buildings to see this magnificent city from above. The view is quite amazing.

PASSAGE E: City of the Rising Sun

21. Which phrase gives a clue to the meaning of *hub* as it is used in paragraph 3?

(A) "For Japan"

(B) "the center"

(C) "many schools"

(D) "two busy airports"

22. This question has two parts. Answer Part A. Then answer Part B.

PART A

What is the main idea of this passage?

(A) Tokyo is a very large and busy city.

(B) Long ago, Edo was a fishing village.

(C) The village of Edo grew over the years.

(D) There are so many things to do in Tokyo.

PART B

Which sentence best supports the answer to Part A?

(A) "Japan has four main islands and hundreds of smaller ones."

(B) "Its name was changed to Tokyo."

(C) "More than 38 million people live there."

(D) "In the center of the city sits the Imperial Palace."

23. What country is Tokyo's nearest neighbor?

(A) China

(B) England

(C) United States

(D) South Korea

24. Why is January 2 a special day in Tokyo?

(A) Baseball season starts.

(B) The Olympic Games begin.

(C) The Emperor gives a speech.

(D) People celebrate the New Year.

25. Which sentence from the last paragraph best supports the idea that Tokyo is a beautiful city? Write the sentence.

_____

_____

ANSWER KEY

WHAT'S A PANGOLIN? (page 6)

1. D

A: Incorrect. The passage says a pangolin is about the size of a dog but does not note any other similarities.

B: Incorrect. The passage says that a pangolin in danger releases a strong smell, like a skunk, but does not note any other similarities.

C: Incorrect. The pangolin eats mostly termites and ants, but it is not like a termite.

D: Correct. The pangolin eats ants and is also called a scaly anteater.

2. B, E

A: Incorrect. Although some pangolins live on the ground, the passage does not say they run from danger.

B: Correct. When in danger, the pangolin rolls into a ball.

C: Incorrect. Although some pangolins live in trees, the passage does not say they climb up a tree to escape from danger.

D: Incorrect. Although some pangolins live in burrows, the passage does not say they go underground to escape from danger.

E: Correct. Like a skunk, a pangolin releases a strong smell to drive enemies away.

3. Medicine (Paragraph 4 says that some people sell pangolin scales, "which people in some countries use for medicine.")

HELLO, ROBOT! (page 7)

1. Alabama (The first sentence says that Ms. Dali is a teacher in Alabama.)

2. D

A: Incorrect. Although Ms. Dali may buy food, the passage is about her buying school supplies.

B: Incorrect. Ms. Dali may buy new clothes, but the passage is about her buying school supplies.

C: Incorrect. Although Ms. Dali may buy books, the passage is about her buying school supplies.

D: Correct. The passage tells how Ms. Dali buys supplies for her classroom.

3. A

A: Correct. The picker robot goes into action when Ms. Dali places her order.

B: Incorrect. The picker robot reaches with its metal arm, but this is not what makes the robot start working.

C: Incorrect. Although Ms. Dali gets ready for school by buying supplies, placing the order is what makes the robot start working.

D: Incorrect. The box of supplies goes onto a truck, but this is not what makes the robot start working.

4. "This robot finds a box that is just the right size. It puts the items into the box." (The third and fourth sentences explain what the packer robot does.)

5. D

A: Incorrect. The box goes from the airport to the school by van, but it goes from Utah to Alabama by plane.

B: Incorrect. Robots use a cart to fill the order, but the box goes to Alabama by plane.

C: Incorrect. A truck carries the box to the airport, but it goes from Utah to Alabama by plane.

D: Correct. The box goes from Utah to Alabama by plane.

WHAT MAKES A CHAMPION? (page 9)

1. B

A: Incorrect. The U.S. Open is held in New York every year, but that's not where Coco was born.

B: Correct. Paragraph 2 says that Coco Gauff was born in in Florida.

C: Incorrect. Coco played at Wimbledon, which is in England, but that's not where she was born.

D: Incorrect. Coco won the junior girls' title in the French Open, but she wasn't born in France.

2. Coco wanted to be the best tennis player in the world. (The first paragraph says that Coco had known this was what she wanted to be since she was 8 years old.)

3. A

A: Correct. Paragraph 3 says that Coco's father is her coach.

B: Incorrect. Although her mother helped Coco in other ways, she is not Coco's coach.

C: Incorrect. The passage does not mention Coco's brother; her father is her coach.

D: Incorrect. Although Venus Williams was one of Coco's heroes, she is not Coco's coach.

4. "Would she be able to handle life in the spotlight?" (The third sentence in the paragraph notes that Coco's parents wondered if she would be able to handle all of the attention she would get "in the spotlight.")

5. B

A: Incorrect. Although most players want to win every game, Coco's goal at Wimbledon was to play her best.

B: Correct. Paragraph 6 says that Coco's goal was to play her best.

C: Incorrect. Although Venus Williams was one of Coco's heroes, beating her was not Coco's goal at Wimbledon.

D: Incorrect. Coco met and even played some well-known players at Wimbledon, but her goal was to play her best.

WHAT DO PRESIDENTS EAT? (page 11)

1. D

A: Incorrect. Paragraph 2 says that presidents often have important guests, but this is a detail in the passage and not the main idea.

B: Incorrect. Although readers might infer that foods have changed since the 1800s, this is not the main idea of the passage.

C: Incorrect. Paragraph 2 says that presidents sometimes plan fancy meals for guests, but it does not say that presidents like fancy foods themselves.

D: Correct. The whole passage tells about the surprising foods that some presidents choose to eat.

2. James Madison liked to serve oyster ice cream, and Dwight Eisenhower served green turtle soup. (Other foods mentioned in the passage were eaten by presidents but not necessarily served to their guests.)

3.

President	cottage cheese	grits	jellybeans	squirrel stew
Jimmy Carter		X		
Gerald Ford	X			
James A. Garfield				X
Richard Nixon	X			
Ronald Reagan			X	

4. C

A: Incorrect. Although the passage says that Eisenhower liked to cook, it does not say that Lincoln did.

B: Incorrect. Although the passage mentions that Eisenhower made soup, it does not say whether or not Lincoln ate soup.

C: Correct. The last paragraph says that Lincoln didn't care much about food and often forgot to eat.

D: Incorrect. Although the passage says that some presidents went to the White House kitchen, it does not say where Lincoln ate his meals.

5. "They plan fancy meals to show off the best American foods." (The third sentence in the paragraph explains that presidents choose certain menu items to "show off the best American foods.")

THE CHANGING COAST GUARD (page 13)

1. C

A: Incorrect. Paragraph 3 says that the USCG was originally called the Revenue Cutter Service, but this is a detail in the passage and not the main idea.

B: Incorrect. Although this is an accurate description of the Coast Guard, it is a general statement and not the main idea.

C: Correct. The passage focuses on changes in the Coast Guard and how its name has changed accordingly.

D: Incorrect. Paragraphs 4 and 5 say that the USCG helps protect ships, but this is a detail and not the main idea.

2. To catch smugglers (Paragraph 3 explains that the main job of the Revenue Cutter Service was to catch smugglers.)

3. A

A: Correct. Paragraph 4 describes how life-saving services became a part of the Coast Guard's job.

B: Incorrect. Although the paragraph mentions "ships at sea," this is a detail and not the main topic.

C: Incorrect. Although the paragraph describes some of the tools used for rescues, this is a detail and not the main topic.

D: Incorrect. Cutters are described in paragraph 3, but this is not a main topic in paragraph 4.

4. C, D

A: Incorrect. Maps are mentioned in paragraph 5 in relation to the modern Coast Guard, but there is no reason to think that the Coast Guard did not have maps earlier.

B: Incorrect. The Coast Guard had cutters from the beginning in 1790.

C: Correct. The last paragraph says that today's Coast Guard has planes as well as ships. Earlier services did not have planes.

D: Correct. The last paragraph says that today's Coast Guard uses helicopters. Earlier services did not have helicopters.

E: Incorrect. Paragraph 5 says that America has had lighthouses since 1716.

5. "They work on lakes and rivers, too, not just on the sea." (Teaching people about safe boating takes place on all bodies of water, including lakes and rivers.)

WILD PONIES OF CHINCOTEAGUE (page 15)

1. C

A: Incorrect. This sentence gives a detail about pony penning, but it is not the main idea.

B: Incorrect. This sentence states an important idea, but it is not the main idea for the whole passage.

C: Correct. The passage focuses on the Chincoteague pony festival.

D: Incorrect. This sentence gives a detail about the ponies on Assateague Island, but it is not the main idea.

2. The ponies may have come from a Spanish ship that wrecked in the 1500s or they may have been brought there to graze by farmers in the 1700s. (Paragraph 1 says that the ponies originally came from either a Spanish shipwreck or local farmers.)

3. "They needed to raise money for a new fire engine." (This sentence tells how the auction came about.)

4. B

A: Incorrect. The first sentence mentions parking, but this is a detail and not the main topic.

B: Correct. The sidebar tells visitors to the festival what they need to know.

C: Incorrect. Although the sidebar advises wearing old clothes and shoes, this is a detail and not the main topic.

D: Incorrect. The main passage describes selling ponies, but the sidebar does not tell where to buy one.

FRANKENSTORM! (page 17)

1. C

A: Incorrect. This sentence tells how computers were used to predict the hurricane's path, but not why it was so powerful.

B: Incorrect. This sentence tells what people called the storm because it happened around Halloween, but it does not explain why the storm was so powerful.

C: Correct. Paragraph 4 explains that Sandy became powerful because it was 900 miles across and the tides were high.

D: Incorrect. This sentence tells when the hurricane struck, but not why it was so powerful.

2. Out to the Atlantic Ocean (Paragraphs 1 and 3 say that U.S. computer models predicted the storm would move out to sea.)

3. "Sandy caused more than $70 billion in damages and claimed many lives." (The last sentence describes what happened as a result of the storm.)

4. B

A: Incorrect. This sentence tells why the tides were high, but it does not explain why people were unprepared for the storm.

B: Correct. People did not prepare for the storm because scientists predicted it would go out to sea.

C: Incorrect. This sentence tells how large the storm was, but it does not explain why people were unprepared for it.

D: Incorrect. This sentence misstates information from the passage: The old computers did not work well in predicting the storm, so weather centers got new ones.

TAMING A RIVER (page 19)

1. B

A: Incorrect. Although the dam would generate power for homes and factories, this was not the reason the government decided to build it.

B: Correct. Paragraph 1 explains that the Colorado River often flooded and caused serious destruction, so a dam was needed to control the flow of water.

C: Incorrect. Although this statement is true, creating jobs was not the reason the government decided to build the dam.

D: Incorrect. Water from snow melt in the Rocky Mountains flows into the Colorado River, but this was not the reason the government decided to build the dam.

2. A

A: Correct. Paragraph 4 says that workers needed a place to live while building the dam, so they built Boulder City.

B: Incorrect. Workers cooled the concrete during dam construction, not before the building began.

C: Incorrect. Workers made stacks of concrete blocks as part of the dam construction, not before the building began.

D: Incorrect. Workers put pipes in the concrete blocks during dam construction, not before the building began.

3. The workers blasted tunnels through rock walls to make the river flow in other directions. (Paragraph 5 explains that workers built tunnels and diverted the river through the tunnels.)

4. B

A: Incorrect. The building of the dam itself created a lake, but this is not why workers forced ice water through pipes in the dam.

B: Correct. Paragraph 6 explains that workers forced ice water through pipes in the dam to cool the concrete.

C: Incorrect. The building of the dam slowed down the river, but this is not why workers forced ice water through the pipes.

D: Incorrect. Workers used grout to seal spaces between the blocks, but forcing ice water through the pipes was not part of that process.

5. C

A: Incorrect. The dam helped control the flow of the river, but it did not stop snow from melting.

B: Incorrect. Although the Colorado River sometimes dried up in summer before the dam was built, the dam did not make some parts of the river dry.

C: Correct. The last paragraph explains that the dam created Lake Mead, which enabled engineers to control the flow of the river.

D: Incorrect. Although the dam project created many jobs, this was not how the dam fixed the problems caused by flooding.

"KOALA! FIND!" (page 21)

1. A

A: Correct. Paragraph 2 states that Australia was very hot and very dry, and paragraph 3 says the winds spread the fires. The reader can infer that these conditions made the fires worse.

B: Incorrect. Paragraph 2 says that summer starts in December, but the passage does not say exactly when the fires started.

C: Incorrect. This was a result of the fires, not a cause.

D: Incorrect. This was an effect of widespread fires, not a cause.

2. "There was nothing on the sand that would burn." (The last sentence explains that the beaches were safe because there was nothing there that would burn.)

3. C

A: Incorrect. The passage says that people helped save koalas, but they did not move them to beaches.

B: Incorrect. The dogs were already trained to find injured animals, so they were not used to find koalas because they needed practice.

C: Correct. Paragraph 5 explains that there was no food for the koalas; they were hungry and frightened.

D: Incorrect. People found animals along the roads at first, but the passage does not say people took dogs to the bushland because there were no more animals on the roads.

4A. B

A: Incorrect. The rescuers may have taken pictures of koalas, but the passage does not say they used cameras to find them.

B: Correct. Trained dogs found the koalas by smell and alerted their handlers.

C: Incorrect. Rescuers may have climbed trees to reach the koalas once they were located, but they did not climb trees to find koalas.

D: Incorrect. Dogs helped locate the koalas by smell but did not drive the koalas out of the trees.

4B. C

A: Incorrect. This sentence describes what one dog was trained to do, but it does not support the idea that the dogs located koalas by smell.

B: Incorrect. This sentence describes what the handlers did during the search, but it does not support the idea that the dogs located koalas by smell.

C: Correct. This sentence supports the idea that the dogs located koalas by smell.

D: Incorrect. This sentence describes what the koalas did, but it does not support the idea that the dogs located koalas by smell.

VISITING MARS (page 23)

1. B

A: Incorrect. The rovers were sent to study Mars, but the scientists used computers to control the rovers.

B: Correct. The context suggests that scientists on Earth controlled the rovers' movements by using computers.

C: Incorrect. The scientists were on Earth, but they used computers to control the rovers.

D: Incorrect. The wheels helped the rovers move around, but scientists used computers to control the rovers.

2. "traveled around Mars and sent back many pictures" (In this context, the word *exploration* refers to moving around and exploring, or looking at, a place.)

3. D

A: Incorrect. The rovers were sent to Mars but operated, or worked, when they got there.

B: Incorrect. The paragraph says that the rovers took soil samples, but that is not the meaning of *operated*.

C: Incorrect. The life of one rover ended in 2019, but *operated* means almost the opposite.

D: Correct. In this context, the word *operated* means "ran" or "worked."

4. A

A: Correct. In this context, the word *mission* refers to the "job" a rover is supposed to do.

B: Incorrect. The word *mission* refers to what the rover is supposed to do, not the rover itself.

C: Incorrect. The rover will take samples of the soil on Mars, but this is only part of the rover's mission.

D: Incorrect. The word *mission* refers to what the rover is supposed to do, not the vehicle itself.

5. C

A: Incorrect. Although the rover may have been turned on when it got to Mars, that is not the meaning of *launched*.

B: Incorrect. Although the rover was planned for years earlier, that happened long before the rover was launched, or sent into space.

C: Correct. In this context, the word *launched* means "sent into space."

D: Incorrect. Although the rover was built for a purpose, that is not the meaning of *launched*.

THE GREAT SPHINX (page 25)

1. C

A: Incorrect. Artists created the Sphinx by carving stone, but this is not the meaning of *archaeologists*.

B: Incorrect. Workers may have helped build the Sphinx, but this is not the meaning of *archaeologists*.

C: Correct. The passage is about an ancient piece of art that archaeologists study, so *archaeologists* must be people who study ancient things.

D: Incorrect. Although scientists study the Sphinx and it is in another country, this is not the meaning of *archaeologists*.

2. B

A: Incorrect. Although a large city may be part of a civilization, that is not the meaning of the word.

B: Correct. As people settled in one place—such as Egypt—and developed a way of life as a group, they created a civilization.

C: Incorrect. Although every civilization has a form of government, that is not the meaning of the word.

D: Incorrect. Although land used for farming may provide food for a civilization, that is not the meaning of the word.

3. D

A: Incorrect. In this context, the word *great* describes a work of art, but *noble* refers to a person of royalty, such as a king or queen.

B: Incorrect. In this context, the word *example* refers to the Sphinx as a work of art, but *noble* refers to a person of royalty.

C: Incorrect. The word *statue* is another word for the Sphinx as a piece of art, but *noble* refers to a person of royalty.

D: Correct. The word *noble* refers to a person of the ruling class, such as a king or queen, who can also be described as "royal."

4. "to honor" (The context clearly suggests that the Great Sphinx was built to honor King Khafre.)

5. "prediction" (A *prophecy* is a description of something that is supposed to happen in the future, or a prediction.)

THE GREATEST OUTDOOR SHOW ON EARTH (page 27)

1. B

A: Incorrect. Although farm tools might be part of exhibits, this is not the meaning of the word.

B: Correct. In this context, the exhibits are shows of farm products.

C: Incorrect. Although *classes* could fit in the context of the sentence, this is not the meaning of the word.

D: Incorrect. Farm helpers might be involved in the exhibits, but this is not the meaning of the word.

2. D

A: Incorrect. Cowboys and cowgirls "compete" for prizes, but this phrase does not give a clue to the meaning of *value*.

B: Incorrect. Cowboys and cowgirls enter "rodeo events," but this phrase does not give a clue to the meaning of *value*.

C: Incorrect. This phrase refers to the prizes but does not help a reader understand the meaning of *value*.

D: Correct. The phrase "two million dollars" suggests that the value of the prizes is a dollar amount, so the word must mean "worth."

3. "skill and strength" (The word *athletic* refers to activities that require skill and strength.)

4. C

A: Incorrect. Although riders must hold on to the bull or horse they are riding, this is not the meaning of *wrestle*.

B: Incorrect. Although the steer may roll over as the cowboy pulls it down, this is not the meaning of *wrestle*.

C: Correct. The context of the sentence suggests that *wrestle* means "pull down"; the steer must be pulled down to the ground.

D: Incorrect. The passage mentions calf roping, but wrestling a steer to the ground involves pulling it down, not tying it with rope.

5. B

A: Incorrect. This phrase refers to the length of the Stampede; it does not give a clue to the meaning of *tourists*.

B: Correct. The phrase "to see the sights" suggests that *tourists* are people who visit places to see things.

C: Incorrect. Although tourists may have fun, the word refers to people who travel to see things.

D: Incorrect. This phrase refers to the popularity of the Stampede; it does not give a clue to the meaning of *tourists*.

A BURIED CITY (page 29)

1. B

A: Incorrect. Although the eruption of Mt. Vesuvius caused many problems, this is not the text structure used in the passage.

B: Correct. Most of this passage describes the effects of the volcanic eruption, which was the cause of what followed.

C: Incorrect. Although the passage gives information about the eruption of Mt. Vesuvius and what happened afterward, it does not ask any questions.

D: Incorrect. Although the passage describes what life was like in Pompeii long ago, it does not compare it to life today.

2. A, C

A: Correct. Paragraph 2 says that the eruption sent clouds of ash into the air, which blocked the sunlight and darkened the sky.

B: Incorrect. When the volcano erupted, people tried to run away from Pompeii, not toward it.

C: Correct. Paragraph 2 says that most people did not escape from the city; they died as a result of the eruption.

D: Incorrect. Paragraph 5 says that scientists found loaves of bread in an oven, but a baker did not put them there because of the eruption.

E: Incorrect. The last paragraph implies that the government opened the city to historians and visitors, but there is no evidence that the government ever closed Pompeii as a result of the eruption.

3. D

A: Incorrect. Some people tried to return to Pompeii, so they did not stop living there because they were afraid of another eruption.

B: Incorrect. People may have lost their property as a result of the eruption, but the passage does not suggest that they stopped living there because they had no money.

C: Incorrect. Some paintings were probably destroyed and others were found undamaged, but people did not stop living in Pompeii because of the paintings.

D: Correct. Paragraph 3 says that some people went back to Pompeii after the eruption but could not dig through the layers of ash, so they left the city forever.

4. "Because the objects under the hard ash were protected from rain and sunlight, they stayed in excellent shape." (This sentence clearly explains that the ash hardened and protected the items underneath it.)

5. B

A: Incorrect. People may have searched for coins and jewelry in Pompeii at one time, but today they go there to see what life was like long ago.

B: Correct. Today, people visit Pompeii to see what life was like long ago.

C: Incorrect. People visit Pompeii to see what life was like long ago, not to watch the volcano erupt again.

D: Incorrect. Visitors can see what the shops, restaurants, and markets looked like long ago, but they can't enjoy them as customers.

FLIPPING FOR SIMONE BILES (page 31)

1. B

A: Incorrect. Although Simone grew up in Texas, that is not what got her interested in gymnastics.

B: Correct. Paragraph 3 says that Simone went on a field trip to a gymnastics center when she was 6, and that sparked her interest in gymnastics.

C: Incorrect. Simone practiced her gymnastics at home as a result of her interest, but that was not what first got her interested.

D: Incorrect. Simone copied the older kids when she visited the gymnastics center, but that was a result of her interest, not the cause.

2A. A

A: Correct. Most of the passage presents information about Simone Biles in time order, from her birth in 1997 to the present.

B: Incorrect. Although the passage mentions some causes of her interest in gymnastics and some effects of her practice, this is not the main text structure used in the passage.

C: Incorrect. Although some texts state a problem and then the solution, this is not the text structure used in the passage.

D: Incorrect. In a way the passage does compare Simone Biles to all other gymnasts, but this is not the main text structure used in the passage.

2B. C, D

A: Incorrect. This sentence compares Simone Biles to other gymnasts, but it does not show time order.

B: Incorrect. This sentence gives a detail about how Simone Biles became a gymnast, but it does not show time order.

C: Correct. This detail sentence supports the time order structure by giving a date.

D: Correct. This sentence supports the time order structure by telling when something happened.

E: Incorrect. Although this sentence uses the word *first*, it does not show time order.

3. D

A: Incorrect. Biles won first place in the all-around event during the World Championship, not after it.

B: Incorrect. Biles was home-schooled before she won the World Championship, not after it.

C: Incorrect. Biles took gymnastics lessons before she won the World Championship, not after it.

D: Correct. Biles won five medals at the Olympics in 2016, which was after she won her first World Championship in 2013.

ARE WE THERE YET? (page 33)

1. To find food; to give birth (Paragraph 3 explains that most animals migrate to find food or give birth.)

2. B

A: Incorrect. Although this section mentions seasons of the year, it does not present information in time order.

B: Correct. Most of this section explains the causes of migration and what happens as a result.

C: Incorrect. This section explains why animals migrate, but it does not present migration as a problem or a solution.

D: Incorrect. Although this section tells about one way turtles and some fish are alike, it does not use comparison and contrast as the text structure.

3A. D

A: Incorrect. Although this section mentions animals traveling every year, it does not present information in time order.

B: Incorrect. Earlier parts of the passage explain the causes of migration, but this section compares the distances traveled by various animals.

C: Incorrect. This section compares the distances traveled by various animals but does not present migration as a problem or a solution.

D: Correct. In this section, the author compares the migration habits of various animals to identify the one that travels farthest.

3B. C

A: Incorrect. This sentence gives the main idea of the section but does not offer a comparison or contrast.

B: Incorrect. This sentence gives a detail about Canada geese but does not offer a comparison or contrast.

C: Correct. This sentence compares the leatherback's migration to that of loggerhead turtles.

D: Incorrect. This sentence gives an opinion about the leatherback's migration but does not offer a comparison or contrast.

4. D

A: Incorrect. The passage says that some birds eat insects and caterpillars, but butterflies do not.

B: Incorrect. The passage says that some fish use a sense of smell to find their way, but birds and butterflies do not.

C: Incorrect. The passage says that some fish and sea turtles lay eggs where they were born, but it does not say that birds and butterflies do this.

D: Correct. Paragraph 5 says that birds and butterflies both use the earth's magnetic pull to find their way.

5. B

A: Incorrect. The passage says that penguins swim a few hundred miles, but this is not the longest migration distance.

B: Correct. The last paragraph says that the Arctic tern has the longest migration.

C: Incorrect. The passage says that Canada geese fly several hundred miles, but this is not the longest migration distance.

D: Incorrect. Loggerhead sea turtles may swim 8,000 miles across the Pacific Ocean, but this is not the longest migration distance.

CIVIL WAR BASEBALL GAME/LETTER FROM A SOLDIER (page 36)

1. D

A: Incorrect. The writer refers to "our brave Union soldiers," but there is no evidence to suggest that he was a soldier himself.

B: Incorrect. The writer reports on a game played in Hilton Head, but there is no evidence to suggest that he lived there.

C: Incorrect. The writer describes baseball in favorable terms, so there is no reason to infer that he did not like baseball.

D: Correct. The reader can infer that the writer was not at the game because the story was printed in Baltimore, he refers to reports about the crowd, and he does not know what the final score was.

2. D

A: Incorrect. Both writers report that the game took place on Christmas Day.

B: Incorrect. The soldier mentions the fire wagon in Text B, but the newspaper report does not mention it.

C: Incorrect. Both writers report that the players were from New York regiments.

D: Correct. The news report says that the game was played in Hilton Head, but the soldier does not tell where it took place or where he was at the time.

3. C

A: Incorrect. The writer of Text A says that one team wore red pants, but neither writer tells who won the game.

B: Incorrect. The writer of Text B says that the food that day was good, but the writer of Text A does not mention food.

C: Correct. Both writers describe baseball as a new sport that is starting to catch on.

D: Incorrect. The writer of Text A describes the colorful uniforms of one team, but the writer of Text B does not mention the uniforms.

4. "I sure enjoyed watching the game." (In paragraph 4, the writer of Text B says he "enjoyed watching the game.")

THE OPENING OF THE GOLDEN GATE BRIDGE/WALKING ACROSS THE NEW BRIDGE (page 38)

1A. C

A: Incorrect. The writer of Text A reports on the opening, but there is no evidence that he helped plan it.

B: Incorrect. The writer of Text A reports from Washington, DC, so he did not watch the opening of the bridge in San Francisco.

C: Correct. Text A is a report filed from Washington, DC, so the writer was not in San Francisco at the opening.

D: Incorrect. The writer of Text A reports the numbers of cars and trucks that crossed the bridge, but he was not there to drive one across.

1B. "Here in Washington, 3,000 miles away, President Roosevelt sent a telegram declaring the bridge open." (This sentence clearly shows that the writer was in Washington, DC, and was not at the opening of the bridge in San Francisco.)

2. D

A: Incorrect. Both texts say Thursday was when people crossed the bridge..

B: Incorrect. Both texts describe the huge crowd at the opening of the bridge.

C: Incorrect. Both writers mention that the bridge was painted orange.

D: Correct. The writer of Text A reports that more than 32,000 vehicles crossed the bridge on Friday, but the writer of Text B does not mention cars or trucks.

3. B, D

A: Incorrect. This sentence tells that the writer woke up early that day but does not indicate where she was.

B: Correct. This sentence shows that the writer was at the opening because she could see the top of the bridge.

C: Incorrect. This sentence describes the bridge but does not indicate where the writer was.

D: Correct. This sentence shows that the writer was at the opening because she stood near the side and looked down at the water.

E: Incorrect. This sentence describes what people did in a general way but does not indicate where the writer was.

4. Possible answers: "Thursday was the most exciting day we've had since moving here to San Francisco." "But it was worth every penny!" (The first and last sentences of the text show that the writer was clearly thrilled to see the new bridge.)

5. A

A: Correct. Text A is a news report from Washington, DC, but Text B is a personal narrative written by a person who was at the opening.

B: Incorrect. Both texts describe the bridge, so this is not a difference.

C: Incorrect. Both texts note that the bridge is in San Francisco, so this is not a difference.

D: Incorrect. Both texts describe the crowd, so this is not a difference.

FIRST LADY OF THE AIR/HARRIET QUIMBY'S DESCRIPTION OF HER FLIGHT (page 41)

1A. A

A: Correct. The way the author describes Quimby suggests that he admires her.

B: Incorrect. There is no evidence to suggest that the author does not like Quimby.

C: Incorrect. Although the author notes that there were no women pilots before Quimby, there is no evidence to suggest that he feels sorry for her.

D: Incorrect. Although the author notes that Quimby decided on her own to fly across the channel, there is no evidence to suggest that he thinks she was selfish.

1B. D

A: Incorrect. This sentence gives information about the first airplane flight but does not support the idea that the author admires Quimby.

B: Incorrect. This sentence gives factual information about Quimby but does not show that the author admires her.

C: Incorrect. This sentence gives information about what Quimby did as a pilot but does not show that the author admires her.

D: Correct. Describing Quimby as a woman of "daring and skill" supports the idea that the author admires her.

2. B

A: Incorrect. This sentence tells when Quimby began flying but does not describe something she was the first person to do.

B: Correct. This sentence describes something Quimby was the first person to do.

C: Incorrect. Although the "idea" refers to Quimby's flight across the Channel, this sentence does not actually describe what she did.

D: Incorrect. This sentence tells what another pilot did but does not describe something Quimby was the first person to do.

3. C

A: Incorrect. This sentence describes the scene as Quimby took off but does not tell how she felt.

B: Incorrect. This sentence describes Quimby's view as she flew along but does not tell how she felt.

C: Correct. This sentence describes how Quimby felt when she saw the shore of France.

D: Incorrect. This sentence describes what Quimby did when she landed but does not tell how she felt.

4. Fishermen (The last paragraph of Text B says that a "crowd of fishermen" ran toward her, and they were speaking French.)

A LONE STAR (page 44)

1. Near El Paso (The timeline shows that the first Spanish settlement was near El Paso in 1682.)

2. C

A: Incorrect. This sentence says that European explorers went to Texas but does not tell why.

B: Incorrect. This sentence describes what de Vaca did, but it does not tell why.

C: Correct. This sentence explains why the first Spanish explorers went to Texas: they were looking for gold.

D: Incorrect. This sentence describes what the explorers found in Texas but does not tell why they went there.

3. Mexico (Paragraph 3 says that Texas was part of Mexico.)

4. D

A: Incorrect. The timeline says that the Alamo was built in 1718, but that is not how Texans won their freedom.

B: Incorrect. The timeline says that Americans began settling in Texas (which was part of Mexico) in 1823, but that is not how they won their freedom.

C: Incorrect. The timeline says that Texas joined the U.S. in 1845, but that is not how they won their freedom.

D: Correct. The timeline says that Texans won their freedom in 1836; paragraph 4 explains that they did so by winning a war against Mexico.

5. "When Texas became its own country, it created a new flag. It had one star." (Texas is called the Lone Star State because its flag has one star. That flag first represented Texas when it was an independent country.)

A SIDE OF ANT EGGS (page 46)

1. D

A: Incorrect. Although this sentence describes a view of American foods, it is not the main idea of the passage.

B: Incorrect. This sentence gives an opinion about foods in China, but it is a detail and not the main idea of the passage.

C: Incorrect. This sentence makes a statement about the foods listed in the chart, but it is not the main idea of the passage.

D: Correct. The main point of this passage is that people in different parts of the world eat different kinds of food.

2. Silkworm pupae, or cocoons (Paragraph 2 says what *beondegi* are.)

3. B

A: Incorrect. Although the passage describes unusual foods eaten in China, the chart does not list any.

B: Correct. The chart lists escargot, or snails, as a food eaten in France.

C: Incorrect. The chart shows that guinea pig is a food in Chile, but snails are eaten in France.

D: Incorrect. The chart shows that ant eggs are eaten in Mexico, but snails are eaten in France.

4. C

A: Incorrect. Although the passage describes some kinds of seafood, the chart says that durian is a fruit.

B: Incorrect. The chart says that cuy is guinea pig, but durian is a fruit.

C: Correct. The chart describes durian as a "smelly fruit."

D: Incorrect. The chart says that a tarantula is a large spider, but durian is a fruit.

5. A, D

A: Correct. Paragraph 4 says that in Mexico, ant eggs are found only in the roots of agave plants.

B: Incorrect. The chart says that tarantulas are large spiders eaten in Cambodia, but it does not say they are found only in certain plants.

C: Incorrect. Paragraph 4 says that *percebes* are sea creatures in shells; they are found in the ocean on rocks, not in plants.

D: Correct. Paragraph 4 says that in the Philippines, woodworms are found only in dead mangrove trees.

E: Incorrect. Paragraph 3 says that fried scorpions are eaten in China, but it does not say that they are found in plants.

6. B

A: Incorrect. Although paragraph 1 mentions corn dogs, there is no evidence to suggest that most Americans eat them.

B: Correct. It is clear from the information in this passage that people eat many different kinds of food.

C: Incorrect. Although the passage says that some foods can be found only at certain times, there is no evidence to support the conclusion that some foods are eaten only once a year.

D: Incorrect. This sentence states an opinion, which some people may agree with, but it is not a conclusion that can be drawn from the passage.

MAN OVERBOARD! (page 49)

1. B

A: Incorrect. The men knew where their lobster traps were, but they had a long trip to get there.

B: Correct. The first paragraph says that the men wanted to empty their lobster traps in the morning, but the traps were many miles from shore.

C: Incorrect. The men planned to empty their lobster traps the next morning; they did not have to empty them right away.

D: Incorrect. There is no evidence to suggest that the men went out on the boat that night because they thought someone would take their lobster traps.

2. A

A: Correct. Paragraph 3 explains that Aldridge filled his rubber boots with air and held them under his arms to stay afloat.

B: Incorrect. Aldridge took his boots off, so they did not keep his feet warm.

C: Incorrect. Aldridge was floating in the ocean, so there was no drinking water to scoop up.

D: Incorrect. Aldridge found a lobster buoy when the sun came up and held on to the buoy, but he did not use his boots to hold on.

3. Sample answer: Near Long Island, NY (The map shows that the search took place off the coast of Long Island, which is part of New York.)

4. "The computer used the information they had to draw a map showing where to look." (A Coast Guard person entered the information they had, and the computer identified where to search.)

5. C

A: Incorrect. The swimmer may have lifted Aldridge by his arms to get him into a rescue basket, but the rescue basket lifted him to the helicopter.

B: Incorrect. Aldridge was already holding on to a buoy when the swimmer found him.

C: Correct. Paragraph 8 states that Bob Hovey put Aldridge in a rescue basket, which was lifted to the helicopter.

D: Incorrect. The helicopter hovered over the spot and lowered a rescue basket.

6. About 12 hours (The times on the map show that Aldridge fell overboard at 3:30 AM and was rescued at 3:12 PM, so he was in the water almost 12 hours.)

DISCOVERING DINO-BIRDS (page 52)

1. B

A: Incorrect. Digging up dinosaur eggs helped scientists verify their theory, but that is not what first led them to think that birds came from dinosaurs.

B: Correct. Finding *Archaeopteryx* made scientists think that birds came from dinosaurs because it was a dinosaur but had wings and feathers.

C: Incorrect. Discovering dinosaur nests helped scientists verify their theory, but that is not what first led them to think that birds came from dinosaurs.

D: Incorrect. Scientists reviewed their conclusions about *Archaeopteryx*, but looking again at old fossils is not what first led them to think that birds came from dinosaurs.

2. "But it also had wings and feathers." (Discoverers of *Archaeopteryx* called it the "first bird" because it had wings and feathers.

3. "This animal had feathers. . . . It walked and ran on two legs as birds do." (Scientists noted that *Deinonychus* had feathers and walked on two legs as birds do.)

4. B

A: Incorrect. This detail says that some dinosaur eggs were like bird eggs, but this did not make scientists think that dinosaurs took care of their young.

B: Correct. Finding male dinosaur fossils next to nests made scientists think that dinosaurs took care of their young.

C: Incorrect. This detail explains that birds take care of their young, but it does not show what made scientists think that dinosaurs took care of their young.

D: Incorrect. This detail describes some changes in dinosaur bodies that took place, but it does not show what made scientists think that dinosaurs took care of their young.

GETTING FROM HERE TO THERE (page 54)

1. A, C

A: Correct. Paragraphs 1 and 3 say that without highways, getting anywhere would take a lot longer.

B: Incorrect. The passage says that traveling would take longer without highways, but it does not say that people could not visit other parts of the country.

C: Correct. Paragraph 1 says that without highways, food from far-off places would spoil before getting to your stores.

D: Incorrect. Driving across the country would take about four days with our highways, not without them.

E: Incorrect. There were few bridges before the highways came along, but bridges big enough for cars and trucks could still be built even if the highways were not.

2A. C

A: Incorrect. The highway system would cost a lot of money to build, so building it would not help pay for new roads and bridges.

B: Incorrect. Although Eisenhower worried about having to face a war, building highways would not prevent an attack from taking place.

C: Correct. Paragraph 3 explains that Eisenhower wanted highways built because he worried the country might face a war or other emergency and highways would help the government take action.

D: Incorrect. Highways would help people drive from coast to coast, but Eisenhower's goal was not to encourage more travel.

2B. "Without highways, moving supplies and troops around would take too long." (Eisenhower knew that, in the event of a war or other emergency, moving supplies and troops around the country would be easier and faster with highways.)

3. A, D

A: Correct. Paragraph 3 says that drivers in 1919 often had to go far out of their way to find a bridge.

B: Incorrect. The description of driving in 1919 does not mention food or difficulties in finding it.

C: Incorrect. Although this may be true to some extent, the passage does not give this reason.

D: Correct. Paragraph 3 says that the roads were terrible and vehicles kept getting stuck.

E: Incorrect. Although this may be true to some extent, the passage does not give this reason.

4. C

A: Incorrect. This sentence supports Eisenhower's view, but it does not show that building the highways was not easy.

B: Incorrect. This sentence tells what Eisenhower did, but it does not show that building the highways was not easy.

C: Correct. Building the highways was not easy because people argued about many things, including about where they should go.

D: Incorrect. This sentence says that everyone came to an agreement eventually, so it does not show that building the highways was not easy.

5. "Both people and products could move quickly to all parts of the country. . . . People could more easily visit other regions." (The last paragraph explains that highways helped unite the country because it helped move goods faster from one part of the country to another and allowed people to travel and visit more places.)

LEARNING FROM HOME (page 57)

1. "They might be sick or live too far away. Something might happen to the school building or the roads so they can't go in. Or some disaster, such as a global pandemic, might force most people to stay home." (These sentences explain reasons why students might have to learn from home.)

2. C

A: Incorrect. Although this sentence helps define what distance learning is, it does not show that distance learning is not new.

B: Incorrect. This sentence helps distinguish distance learning from online learning, but it does not show that distance learning is not new.

C: Correct. This sentence shows that distance learning is not new; it has been around since at least the 1930s.

D: Incorrect. Although this sentence describes what distance learning is like today, it does not show that distance learning is not new.

3A. B

A: Incorrect. The author mentions a number of reasons for distance learning but does not say it should be used only in an emergency.

B: Correct. The author recommends distance learning as an approach that provides more benefits than just learning.

C: Incorrect. Although the author describes some benefits of distance learning, she does not say it is the best approach for everyone.

D: Incorrect. The author says that distance learning does not work well for everyone, but she does not say it makes schoolwork harder for most students.

3B. D

A: Incorrect. This sentence describes a feature of distance learning but does not show that it helps students in more ways than just learning.

B: Incorrect. This sentence describes how teachers can help students learn, but it does not show that distance learning helps students in more ways than just learning.

C: Incorrect. This sentence describes how distance learning can help students learn, but it does not show how it helps students in more ways than just learning.

D: Correct. This sentence describes a way that distance learning helps students in more ways than just learning.

4. C, D

A: Incorrect. This sentence describes a benefit of distance learning, not a problem with depending on technology.

B: Incorrect. This sentence describes some special things students can do with distance learning, not a problem with depending on technology.

C: Correct. Paragraph 7 explains that not having access to a computer can be a problem for distance learning.

D: Correct. Paragraph 7 explains that a weak or unreliable internet connection can be a problem for distance learning.

E: Incorrect. This sentence describes a potential drawback to distance learning, but it is not a problem with depending on technology.

5. D

A: Incorrect. Since distance learning depends on the use of technology, it is not intended to help students become comfortable with technology.

B: Incorrect. The author describes some benefits of distance learning but does not say that students can choose when to do schoolwork.

C: Incorrect. Although paragraphs 5 and 6 describe some benefits of distance learning, the ability to choose teachers is not one of them.

D: Correct. Paragraph 6 explains that distance learning can be beneficial because it allows students to experience things outside of their familiar surroundings.

A FUNNY GUY (page 60)

1. D

A: Incorrect. The sidebar suggests that Dog Man often saves people, but characters in Captain Underpants don't.

B: Incorrect. The passage says that characters in Captain Underpants get into trouble in school, but not the characters in Dog Man.

C: Incorrect. The passage says that one of Pilkey's teachers encouraged him to write books, but it does not say his teachers liked the characters in both series.

D: Correct. Paragraph 4 says that characters in both series are based on the comics Pilkey made up when he was in school.

2. C, D

A: Incorrect. Although Pilkey loves dogs and created a character named Dog Man, the passage does not say that George and Harold like dogs.

B: Incorrect. Although Pilkey went to college, the passage does not say that George and Harold go to college.

C: Correct. Paragraph 4 says that George and Harold like to make silly comics, just as Pilkey did when he was a kid.

D: Correct. Paragraph 4 says that George and Harold have trouble behaving in school, just as Pilkey did when he was a kid.

E: Incorrect. Although George and Harold are the main characters in Captain Underpants, the passage does not say that Pilkey or the characters want to be captains.

3.

	Dog Man	Captain Underpants	Both
It has silly characters.			X
Its main character has superpowers.	X		
It is a graphic novel.	X		
It was made into a movie.		X	

4. A

A: Correct. The sidebar says that Dog Man is Pilkey's favorite character, but the main passage does not say this.

B: Incorrect. Both the passage and the sidebar describe how Pilkey drew cartoons and created comics when he was a child.

C: Incorrect. The passage says that Pilkey had trouble in school, but the sidebar does not mention this.

D: Incorrect. Paragraph 1 says that Dog Man is one of Pilkey's most popular series, but the sidebar does not mention this.

THE GREAT BARRIER REEF (page 62)

1. D

A: Incorrect. Although the Great Barrier Reef is beautiful, it is important because it supports huge numbers of plants and animals.

B: Incorrect. The Great Barrier Reef is a great place to visit, but it is important because it supports huge numbers of plants and animals.

C: Incorrect. Although the Great Barrier Reef can be seen from space, it is important because it supports huge numbers of plants and animals.

D: Correct. Paragraph 5 explains that the Great Barrier Reef supports huge numbers of plants and animals, and that is its greatest importance.

2. B, E

A: Incorrect. Paragraph 2 provides this information, but the sidebar does not.

B: Correct. The sidebar explains this, but the passage does not mention it.

C: Incorrect. Paragraph 2 provides this information, but the sidebar does not.

D: Incorrect. Paragraph 1 provides this information, but the sidebar does not.

E: Correct. The sidebar explains this, but the passage does not mention it.

3. Rising water temperature or climate change (Both the passage and the sidebar explain that bleaching is caused by rising water temperature, a result of climate change.)

4.

	Passage	Sidebar	Both
Healthy coral reefs are colorful.	X		
Over 400 types of coral live in the Great Barrier Reef.	X		
Pollution from cities and farms can harm coral reefs.		X	
Divers can damage the Great Barrier Reef.			X
The Green Fins program teaches people how to dive near coral reefs.	X		

5. C

A: Incorrect. Both the passage and the sidebar provide this information.

B: Incorrect. Both the passage and the sidebar provide this information.

C: Correct. Paragraph 6 mentions this fact, but the sidebar does not mention it.

D: Incorrect. The sidebar mentions this fact, but the passage does not.

MACHU PICCHU (page 65)

1. C

A: Incorrect. This sentence tells when Machu Picchu was built and by whom but does not tell what it looks like.

B: Incorrect. This sentence tells when the Inca people settled in Peru but does not tell what Machu Picchu looks like.

C: Correct. This sentence describes some features of Machu Picchu.

D: Incorrect. This sentence gives an opinion about the building of Machu Picchu but does not tell what it looks like.

2. The Inca people (Paragraph 1 says that the Inca people built Machu Picchu.)

3. B, E

A: Incorrect. Both the passage and the sidebar include this detail.

B: Correct. Only the sidebar provides this information.

C: Incorrect. Both the passage and the sidebar include this detail.

D: Incorrect. The passage provides this information, but the sidebar does not mention it.

E: Correct. Only the sidebar includes this detail.

4. B

A: Incorrect. This sentence describes the location of Machu Picchu, but it does not explain why it was called a "lost city."

B: Correct. This sentence explains that Machu Picchu was a "lost city" because it sat empty for centuries, and few people knew where it was.

C: Incorrect. This sentence describes the weight of the stones used to build Machu Picchu, but it does not explain why it was called a "lost city."

D: Incorrect. This sentence describes Machu Picchu as a tourist destination, but it does not explain why it was called a "lost city."

5. It may have been used as a summer home for the emperor or a place for the Inca to hide from their enemies. (Paragraph 4 gives two possible explanations for why Machu Picchu was built.)

STRONG AND HONEST ABE (page 67)

1. D

A: Incorrect. Paragraph 2 says that Lincoln was very smart, but this is a detail and not the main idea.

B: Incorrect. Paragraph 2 says that Lincoln towered over most men, but this is a detail and not the main idea.

C: Incorrect. The first paragraph says that Lincoln was the 16th President, but this is a detail and not the main idea.

D: Correct. The main idea of the passage is that Lincoln was a good wrestler.

2. "He said that Thompson won fair and square." (Lincoln's friends thought the wrestling match was a draw, but Lincoln was so honest that he admitted he had lost.)

3. C

A: Incorrect. Although Lincoln mentioned a grizzly bear, he was not comparing Thompson to a wild animal.

B: Incorrect. Although Lincoln said that Thompson could throw a grizzly bear, he did not mean that Thompson fought bears.

C: Correct. Lincoln meant that Thompson was so strong he could throw a grizzly bear—a large animal that can weigh several hundred pounds.

D: Incorrect. Although Lincoln said that Thompson could throw a grizzly bear, he did not mean that Thompson liked throwing things.

WHO NEEDS BEES? (page 68)

1. A

A: Correct. Paragraph 1 explains that bees help food grow by spreading pollen from plant to plant.

B: Incorrect. Although bees do use nectar to make honey, this is not how they help food grow.

C: Incorrect. Bees spread pollen from plant to plant, but the passage does not say that they also carry seeds.

D: Incorrect. Although certain plants attract the bees with smells or color, this is not how bees help food grow.

2. "Poisons, plant diseases, changing climate, and other threats are killing our bees." (This sentence explains that bees need our help because they are dying.)

3. B

A: Incorrect. The passage notes that bees are attracted to flowers with bright colors; it does not recommend choosing flowers of all one color.

B: Correct. The directions recommend choosing flowers that will attract bees.

C: Incorrect. The directions recommend flowers that bloom at different times, but they do not say anything about plant height.

D: Incorrect. The passage notes that bees are attracted to flowers with bright colors and interesting smells, not flowers that are large.

4. D

A: Incorrect. Although the directions suggest adding a few stones to a bowl of water, it is the water that's important.

B: Incorrect. The directions suggest providing a bowl of water, but it is the water that's important, not the bowl.

C: Incorrect. Although the directions suggest adding twigs to a bowl of water, it is the water that's important.

D: Correct. In the directions, step 5 says that bees need water in the garden.

ANCIENT FISH IN DANGER (page 70)

1. C

A: Incorrect. Although paragraph 1 mentions this fact, it is a detail and not the main idea.

B: Incorrect. The photo caption provides this information, but it is a detail and not the main idea.

C: Correct. The main idea of the passage is that sturgeons have survived since the time of the dinosaurs.

D: Incorrect. Although paragraph 1 mentions this event, it is a detail and not the main idea.

2. B, C

A: Incorrect. This sentence tells when dinosaurs lived but does not describe the effect of an asteroid hitting Earth.

B: Correct. This sentence describes one effect of an asteroid hitting Earth.

C: Correct. This sentence describes an effect of an asteroid hitting Earth.

D: Incorrect. This sentence mentions an animal that survived the cold and darkness, but it does not describe the effect of an asteroid hitting Earth.

E: Incorrect. This sentence describes sturgeons but not an effect of an asteroid hitting Earth.

3. Worms, mussels, and other things that live in the sand and mud (Paragraph 2 says that sturgeons are bottom-feeders that eat things that live in the sand and mud.)

4. D

A: Incorrect. This sentence tells what happened when an asteroid struck Earth but does not explain why sturgeons were almost wiped out by the 1990s.

B: Incorrect. This sentence suggests in a general way that sturgeons faced some difficulties, but it does not explain why they were almost wiped out by the 1990s.

C: Incorrect. This sentence explains that people like to eat fish eggs, but it does not explain why sturgeons were almost wiped out by the 1990s.

D: Correct. This sentence explains that sturgeons were almost wiped out because people ate so much caviar that few eggs ever hatched.

PRACTICE TEST (page 73)

The practice test has 25 questions for a total of 30 points.

1A. C *[main idea]*

A: Incorrect. Paragraph 4 makes this point, but this is a detail and not the main idea.

B: Incorrect. Paragraph 1 makes this point, but this is a detail and not the main idea.

C: Correct. This is the main idea of the passage, that plants and animals from the ocean can benefit people.

D: Incorrect. Paragraph 1 provides this information, but this is a detail and not the main idea.

1B. D *[main idea and supporting details]*

A: Incorrect. This sentence describes the sea lamprey but does not show how ocean plants and animals can help people.

B: Incorrect. This sentence explains that the sea lamprey can recover from an injury, but it does not show how ocean plants and animals can help people.

C: Incorrect. This sentence explains that human nerves do not grow back when they are damaged, but it does not show how ocean plants and animals can help people.

D: Correct. This sentence gives an example of how ocean plants and animals can help people.

2. Possible responses: pudding, jam, ice cream, shampoo, toothpaste, and paint (Paragraph 3 lists what carrageenan from red seaweed is used to make.) *[details and inferences]*

3. A *[word meaning]*

A: Correct. In this context, the word *produce* means "make," or manufacture. The sentence that follows explains that plastic is made from petroleum.

B: Incorrect. The passage says that people make a lot of plastic but does not mention selling it.

C: Incorrect. Although the word *need* could fit into the sentence, the word *produce* means "make."

D: Incorrect. The word *destroy* could fit into the sentence, but the meaning of *produce* is almost the opposite.

4. B *[relating events and ideas]*

A: Incorrect. This sentence explains what plastic is made from but does not tell why Lucy Hughes invented a new plastic.

B: Correct. This sentence explains that Lucy Hughes invented a new plastic because she wanted to find a way to use fishing waste.

C: Incorrect. This sentence describes the new plastic Lucy Hughes invented but does not tell why she did it.

D: Incorrect. This sentence describes a characteristic of Lucy Hughes's new plastic but does not tell why she invented it.

5. D *[text structure]*

A: Incorrect. Although the passage uses some sequence words, such as "before long," the passage does not present information in time order.

B: Incorrect. The passage presents problems and solutions but does not make any comparisons or contrasts.

C: Incorrect. Although the passage describes some problems and their causes or their effects, the main text structure is problem and solution.

D: Correct. Most of the passage presents a problem and then describes a solution to that problem.

6. D *[relating events and ideas]*

A: Incorrect. Although Jessica Meir grew up in Maine, that is not why she wanted to become an astronaut.

B: Incorrect. Jessica walked in space after she became an astronaut, so that is not what made her dream of becoming one.

C: Incorrect. The photo caption says that Jessica was a pilot before she became an astronaut, but that is not why she wanted to become an astronaut.

D: Correct. Paragraph 1 says that Jessica dreamed of being an astronaut when she looked up at the stars.

7. C *[reasons and evidence]*

A: Incorrect. This sentence describes something impressive that Meir did, but others had spent months in space before she did.

B: Incorrect. Although spending more than six months on the ISS was something special, this was not the first time anyone had done it.

C: Correct. This sentence describes something no one else had done before: a spacewalk conducted by women only.

D: Incorrect. Spending 205 days in space was impressive, but Meir was not the first one to do so.

8. B, E *[details and inferences]*

A: Incorrect. Although the ISS has several connected parts, the passage does not provide this information.

B: Correct. Paragraph 2 says that five space agencies and astronauts from several countries share the ISS.

C: Incorrect. Although this may be true, the passage does not provide this information.

D: Incorrect. Astronauts live and work on the ISS as it orbits Earth, but it does not take astronauts to the moon.

E: Correct. Paragraph 2 says that the ISS has flown for more than 20 years.

9. She was a pilot and an aquanaut. (The photo caption says that Meir was a pilot and an aquanaut, or underwater scientist, before she became an astronaut.) *[interpreting information]*

10. A *[point of view]*

A: Correct. The author's description of Meir as a person who made history and made her dream come true suggests that she admires her.

B: Incorrect. There is no evidence in the passage to suggest that the author dislikes Meir.

C: Incorrect. Although the author implies her admiration for Meir, she does not express pride in her achievements.

D: Incorrect. Although the author may envy Meir, there is no evidence in the passage to support this idea.

11. B *[main idea]*

A: Incorrect. Although paragraph 2 includes this fact, it is a detail and not the main idea.

B: Correct. The entire passage gives an overview of the U.S. space program.

C: Incorrect. Paragraph 3 includes this fact, but it is a detail and not the main idea.

D: Incorrect. Although paragraph 5 provides this information, it is a detail and not the main idea.

12. A *[text structure]*

A: Correct. The passage presents information in chronological order, from 1961 to 2028.

B: Incorrect. Although the passage mentions some causes and effects of NASA programs, the main text structure is time order.

C: Incorrect. Although NASA had to solve problems along the way, the passage presents information mainly in chronological order.

D: Incorrect. The passage describes a new spacecraft, but it does not make any specific comparisons or contrasts to others.

13. The crew module (According to the picture and caption, the astronauts will ride in the crew module.) *[interpreting information]*

14. C *[integrating information]*

A: Incorrect. Passage B mentions astronauts from "several countries" and five space agencies, but only Passage C says that 15 countries helped build the ISS.

B: Incorrect. Passage C gives this information about the history of the space program, but Passage B does not mention it.

C: Correct. Both passages present this information.

D: Incorrect. Passage C makes this statement about Mars, but Passage B does not.

15. *[integrating information]*

Details	Passage B	Passage C	Both
In the Apollo program, people landed on the moon.		X	
Two women walked in space in 2019.	X		
The ISS travels around Earth.			X
The U.S. shares the ISS with other countries.			X
NASA plans to return to the Moon.		X	

16. D *[word meaning]*

A: Incorrect. Although Bill Pickett and his brother started their own show, that is not what *toured* means.

B: Incorrect. Bill Pickett and his brother took their show to county fairs, so they did not follow the fairs.

C: Incorrect. Although Bill Pickett and his brother worked at county fairs, that is not what *toured* means.

D: Correct. The sentence says that Bill Pickett and his brother toured fairs all over two states, so *toured* must mean "traveled to."

17. B *[relating events and ideas]*

A: Incorrect. Although Pickett rode horses in rodeo shows and was certainly good at it, that is not what he became famous for.

B: Correct. Paragraph 2 explains that Pickett invented a trick that involved wrestling bulls and became a star for doing it.

C: Incorrect. Although Pickett became known as a "bull-dogger," the term refers to wrestling bulls and not training dogs.

D: Incorrect. Pickett acted in a movie about himself when he was already famous; the passage does not suggest that he became famous for acting.

18. "The crowds loved him." (This sentence clearly shows that people loved Bill Pickett.) *[point of view]*

19. C *[reasons and evidence]*

A: Incorrect. This sentence tells how bull-dogging was invented, but it does not tell why people enjoyed watching it.

B: Incorrect. This sentence describes bull-dogging but does not tell why people enjoyed watching it.

C: Correct. This sentence explains why people enjoyed bull-dogging.

D: Incorrect. This sentence tells what happened to Pickett as a result of bull-dogging, but it does not tell why people enjoyed watching it.

20. Pickett became the first Black American to be named to the National Cowboy Hall of Fame. *[integrating information]*

21. B *[word meaning]*

A: Incorrect. The word *hub* refers to the center of something, such as a country, but "For Japan" does not give a clue to this meaning.

B: Correct. This phrase, "the center," helps the reader understand that *hub* means the center of something.

C: Incorrect. The passage says that Tokyo has "many schools," but this phrase does not give a clue to the meaning of *hub*.

D: Incorrect. Although the passage says that Tokyo has "two busy airports," this phrase does not give a clue to the meaning of *hub*.

22A. A *[main idea]*

A: Correct. This is the main idea of this passage.

B: Incorrect. Although paragraph 2 includes this fact, it is a detail and not the main idea.

C: Incorrect. Paragraph 2 provides this information, but it is a detail and not the main idea.

D: Incorrect. Although paragraph 5 makes this statement, it is an opinion and not the main idea.

22B. C *[main idea and supporting details]*

A: Incorrect. This sentence describes the land masses that make up Japan, but it does not support the idea that Tokyo is a large and busy city.

B: Incorrect. Although this sentence gives some history about Tokyo, it does not show that Tokyo is a large and busy city.

C: Correct. Having such a large population supports the idea that Tokyo is a large and busy city.

D: Incorrect. This sentence describes a palace in the city, but it does not show that Tokyo is a large and busy city.

23. D *[interpreting information]*

A: Incorrect. The map shows that China lies near Japan to the west, but South Korea is closest to Tokyo.

B: Incorrect. Although England may be a familiar name, it is not shown on the map and is not close to Tokyo.

C: Incorrect. Although the United States also borders the Pacific Ocean, it is not shown on the map and is not close to Tokyo.

D: Correct. The map shows that South Korea is the closest country to Tokyo.

24. C *[relating events and ideas]*

A: Incorrect. Although baseball is very popular in Japan, its season does not start on January 2.

B: Incorrect. Paragraph 5 mentions the Olympics, but the passage does not mention the date the games begin.

C: Correct. Paragraph 4 says that the Emperor gives a speech to the people of Japan every year on January 2.

D: Incorrect. Although some people may celebrate the New Year on January 2, this is not what makes it a special day in Japan.

25. "You can also visit some very tall buildings to see this magnificent city from above." (The next-to-last sentence in the paragraph describes the city as "magnificent," which supports the idea that Tokyo is beautiful.) *[reasons and evidence]*